Praise for *Building the Literacy Block*

"Bridget does a fabulous job giving a plethora of concrete ideas for upper elementary teachers to meaningfully structure their literacy block. Her emphasis on intentional planning, building routines, and putting students in the driver seat of their own learning supports student critical thinking while simultaneously cultivating their love of reading."
        —**Shane Saeed**, Instructional Coach, St Vrain Valley School District

"Every upper elementary literacy teacher can benefit from Bridget Spackman's deep knowledge of effective instruction and the structure, strategies, and specific examples provided in *Building the Literacy Block*!"
        —**Michelle Emerson**, Author of *First Class Teaching*

"Structuring a literacy block is a challenge that is rarely a focus in preparing educators for their time in the classroom. Spackman has done a phenomenal job of using her classroom experience to create a resource that feels like she's sitting next to you and guiding you to literacy success!"
        —**Juan E. Gonzalez, Jr.**, Third Grade Teacher

"*Building the Literacy Block* is the PD you need. Written by a teacher for teachers. Bridget Spackman asks all the right questions that make you take a second and third look at your routines, procedures, and how you teach standards, skills, and strategies. She offers intentional, practical, and effective solutions to bridge reading and writing into a true literacy block. The examples she provides lets you know she is a real, working classroom teacher. Whether you are a first year or veteran teacher, *Building the Literacy Block* is a must for your personal bookshelf."
        —**Lesley Carmichael**, Classroom teacher, Georgia, USA

Building the Literacy Block

the

Literacy Block

Structuring the Ultimate ELA Workshop

Building
the
Literacy Block

Structuring the Ultimate ELA Workshop

Bridget M. Spackman

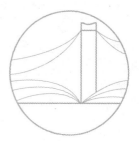

JB JOSSEY-BASS™
A Wiley Brand

Jossey-Bass
A Wiley Imprint
111 River St, Hoboken, NJ 07030
www.josseybass.com

Jossey-Bass books and products are available through most bookstores. To contact Jossey-Bass directly, call our Customer Care Department within the U.S. at 800-956-7739, outside the U.S. at +1 317 572 3986, or fax +1 317 572 4002.

Wiley also publishes its books in a variety of electronic formats and by print-on-demand. Some material included with standard print versions of this book may not be included in e-books or in print-on-demand. If this book refers to media such as a CD or DVD that is not included in the version you purchased, you may download this material at http://booksupport.wiley.com. For more information about Wiley products, visit www.wiley.com.

Library of Congress Cataloging-in-Publication Data

Names: Bridget M. Spackman, author.
Title: Building the literacy block : structuring the ultimate ELA workshop
  / Bridget Spackman.
Description: First edition. | Hoboken, NJ : Jossey-Bass, [2023]
Identifiers: LCCN 2022058891 (print) | LCCN 2022058892 (ebook) | ISBN
  9781119819592 (paperback) | ISBN 9781119819608 (epub) | ISBN
  9781119819615 (adobe pdf)
Subjects: LCSH: Language arts (Elementary) | Literacy.
Classification: LCC LB1576 .S722 2023 (print) | LCC LB1576 (ebook) | DDC
  372.6—dc23/eng/20230125
LC record available at https://lccn.loc.gov/2022058891
LC ebook record available at https://lccn.loc.gov/2022058892

Cover Design: Wiley
Cover Image: © Mohamad Faizal Bin Ramli/Getty Images
Photo taken by: Bridget Spackman

SKY10042655_020923

To my phenomenal husband, Trent Spackman.

Contents

Author's Note

The strategies that will help us run our classrooms are what we go to college to learn. We are told about research-based practices, child development, and cognitive thinking. We can do well on exams. However, understanding how we apply this research to the classroom remains ambiguous. We practice strategies during internships. We see the connections between what we have learned and how to apply it to teaching. Even then, nothing prepares us for the day that we begin our teaching careers and go deep into the trenches of our classroom.

We greet the first year of teaching with stress, feeling overwhelmed with responsibilities and minute tasks, and the need to survive. Most of us don't read research articles or work to understand the science of learning during our first year of teaching. Instead, we turn to coworkers for advice on how to structure our classrooms, resources that work, and strategies that make things easier. As we get more comfortable with our position, we look more critically at the practices we are implementing. This process leads us to research and evaluate the effectiveness of our teaching. However, we receive little guidance on how to apply this research to the everyday classroom. So how do we go about applying the research and continuing to develop what is working in our classrooms? The answer lies in creating connections between our experiences and the research we are reading.

A game of balance is what we experience in teaching and in life. We have to balance the sweets we consume, the tv we binge, and even the amount of work others put on us and we put on ourselves. Identifying the strategies and ideas that we incorporate into our classrooms is another example of how we have to remember to balance everything we do.

It is not practical to dismiss the experiences you have learned; instead, take the research you have collected to reflect and improve on the practices in your classroom. This book is an anecdotal collection of my journey as a teacher. I hope it helps you reflect on your practices and beliefs about what literacy instruction should look and sound like. I hope you use this as an opportunity to create connections between the research you've read and studied and the experiences that I share with you. Remember, there is no one way to structure your literacy block because the 25 students in your classroom have unique personalities and needs.

My career has taken me on a never-ending journey to find methods and practices that are authentic and practical. I have pored over research articles and challenged them with skepticism. I've developed connections to what's happening in the classroom and how it will apply to the world. This book directly results from the years I have spent reading research and doing the work of a public school teacher.

Who Is This Book For?

I am a believer in making sure something is going to benefit me before I put in the time and money. Therefore, I wanted to share who exactly this book is for and the purpose of this book. This book is mainly for upper elementary teachers. While I share some of my kindergarten experiences with you in this book, they provide a context for my viewpoints on education, as well as teaching reading and writing. Some of my biggest learning moments came from when I taught kindergarten and this carried over into upper elementary. As an upper elementary teacher, this book will offer you insights into how to structure your literacy block using various components that are found in an ELA workshop. There are helpful tips for management, organization, and an answer to the famous question, "What do I have my students do during independent work?"

This book serves new and veteran teachers looking to improve the structure of their literacy block. When you get the key to your classroom, you are on a new solo journey. You do the same thing for 180 days before you have a break and fall back into the same routine you were in just two months prior. You can easily become disconnected from the ideas and strategies that are developing in education. This book is an opportunity to learn about strategies for structuring your literacy block and how to implement strategies you may not be familiar with. Even if you're already familiar with the strategies in this book, taking the time to refresh and reconsider them for your classroom is incredibly powerful. It is easy to get stuck in your ways, and this book can bring life and excitement back into your classroom.

The book serves those who want to create an environment that is fun. A coworker of mine tells parents at meet-the-teacher night that she wants to be the teacher that she wants for her boys. I can't agree with her more. Each day, I walk in and imagine my boys sitting in my classroom. What experiences do I want to give them? How do I build an environment that they love and want to come back to every day? This book has ideas, strategies, and tips that will help you create a fun and authentic classroom. Not every teacher has to commit to transforming a classroom or creating a song to hook their students' interest. This book gives you practical suggestions, along with fun games and simple transformation ideas. In the simplest of words, there is something for everyone.

Finally, if you are someone who enjoys a simple and laid-back read that shares experiences and stories, this book is for you! Heavy research, statistics, and deep explanations of cognitive science are important to read about and understand; however, this book is not that. I enjoy reading about the experiences of other teachers when the text has a conversational style and easy-to-follow format, and that's what I have for you in this book. You'll find bullet points, end of the chapter wrap-ups that help you implement the information into your classroom. Join me on the journey to creating your ideal literacy block that creates authentic and rigorous learning opportunities for your students.

Introduction
Been There Done That

There is nothing more rewarding than having your own students push you to be your best. That feeling when they ask questions that go beyond the basic routine of what you do in your classroom and pushes you to *poke the box*; leaving you to question everything. It makes you stronger, and it continues to push education into a more meaningful experience for you and your students. This was the case several years ago when I sat with a group of seven sixth graders at my meeting area. It was a small space in the back of my classroom. I had the typical whiteboard and a small swivel chair to sit in. I surveyed the room to make sure that all the students were working on their assignments. I handed each of the students in my group a new word list and a pack of papers that allowed them to take notes from the Words Their Way Lesson. This was a standard routine in my classroom. My district at the time required learners to have lessons from the program known as Words Their Way, but to help customize the lessons students were placed in groups based on individual assessments. The goal with this entire process was for students to be engaged because we were challenging them and meeting them at the perfect level. However, that day my students blew my mind.

I had always known that spelling tests were not meaningful. There were so many research articles, posts, and leading individuals in the field of education who steered away from spelling tests. This understanding led me to try other forms of word study methods. Words Their Way, a program utilized by my district at the time, was one that I tried to incorporate into my teaching. In order to develop a more meaningful approach with Words Their Way, I decided on a more personalized approach. I separated my class into groups based on the needs of students. Each group would have its own lesson and activities to follow. While I thought this approach was impactful to the learning of my students, one particular group would bring it to my attention that it did not agree. It was a typical instructional day, and as I sat in my chair handing out the word list and packet, I started with the same routine: Students cut out their words and begin looking for a pattern with their elbow partners, an assigned turn-and-talk partner for classroom discussion. After sharing, I gave them specific notes to take and then they would spend a week working on various methods for practicing the spelling pattern. This included the typical things such as: using the words in sentences, speed sorting, rainbow spelling, and other methods. However, on this day, the group of students stopped working and they all looked at one another. Then one student said, "Mrs. Spackman, why do we have to do this?" I felt like a great teacher because I explained how understanding the patterns of words would help them develop their fluency, understand the meanings of words, and decrease spelling errors. I felt like I had nailed that question, but the questions and concerns continued. The next thing I knew my entire group was chiming in and countering my answer. They told me that it was boring, they were just memorizing for the test, and that it felt like busy work.

Ouch. That hit me hard in my teacher's heart. At that very moment, I stopped and listened. I didn't show my feelings of being hurt, and I didn't tell them they were wrong. I sat and listened to how they were feeling. Everything they were sharing sounded completely logical. The more examples they gave, the more I began to question everything we were doing. So, I did what any great teacher would have done, I asked them what we should do differently while still meeting the standards. As you can imagine, this absolutely stunned them. At that moment I could have either: A) told them that there was no other way, therefore we had to keep doing it this way, or B) stopped what we were doing and went back to the drawing board. I'll let y'all guess which one I chose.

I want you to stop and think about how often we consider the purpose behind what we do in the classroom. Why do you have students place certain items in a folder? Why do we start a lesson a particular way? Why do we teach the way we do? When we understand our why, we can be more intentional with our lessons and our time. However, we have to remember that everything we do is not about us. When we create a lesson, we might think it is intentional, authentic, and useful to our students, but if we don't have their buy-in and understanding, then does it matter?

I've taught so many grade levels during my career as a teacher. At the very beginning of my career, I was a kindergarten teacher. During this time, I soaked in everything I could from setting up a classroom to implementing behavior management. Honestly, without this experience I don't know if I would be in the same position I am in today. The school that I taught at was making some big shifts in how they were structuring their reading blocks. They had decided only a year or two prior to step away from using the boxed curriculum to fidelity and really looking at the needs of the students. We started the year off with a good old-fashioned book study as a faculty. The book was called *The Daily 5* by Gail Boushey. During my first and second year of teaching, I used it to help structure every inch of my classroom. I followed the first 20 days, a gradual release model that established the Daily 5 stations, and made sure my rotations were always up to date with the materials we had learned from the week prior.

Things started to shift my third year. At this point, I had a specific routine and process for implementing *The Daily 5*. I had a solid foundation and knew exactly what worked for me and my teaching style. I remember sitting at my kidney table in one corner of my classroom. I had the perfect visual of all my students as they were working on their rotations. Students participated in reading by themselves near the library, worked with words at the tables, and read with partners at the big book station or the pocket chart area. On this day, I got my small group started on something to do. I stood up and walked about the classroom to see how my students were progressing with their work. I noticed that some of them were tapping, rather furiously, at the partner chart. The students at the independent reading station were laying down with the book on their faces, and the kiddos at the word work center were using the dry erase marker to create circles all over the boards.

What happened? How did the hours that I had spent creating and cutting out these centers not engage my students? Was this day just a fluke? Did they need a break? I spent the next month observing my class. During that month I noticed that my students were not engaged. They lacked passion for the centers and my biggest realization was that they were not learning. I resolved to create a well-structured and meaningful block for my kindergarteners. Was it possible?

During my fourth year as a kindergarten teacher, I made big changes in the approach to literacy instruction. I created meaningful integrated activities, established goal setting, and allowed my students to work on literacy projects that they were passionate about. I had students who created author studies, others who researched topics they were passionate about, and opportunities for those students to present to the class. My students grew in ways that I could not have imagined, but my time as a kindergarten teacher would be short lived. That same year my husband and I decided to move from Alabama to Pennsylvania after I accepted a position as a fourth-grade English Language Arts (ELA) teacher. I was excited for the change, but nervous because I had no idea how to establish a reading and writer's workshop at that age.

I read a lot of books that year. In particular, *The Book Whisperer* and *Reading in the Wild* by Donalyn Miller, and *The Reading Strategies Book* by Jennifer Serravallo helped me understand the importance of developing an avid reader. They offered some incredible strategies but they never really articulated what the block of time that I had would look and sound like. My school had limited resources and gave little guidance in how to structure my time. So, I did what most teachers do in this situation, I asked other teachers what they were doing, and I spent hours on social media and the web looking for answers. My first year was a hodgepodge of various strategies and activities. Individually, they all sounded beautiful, but together there was little to no harmony.

I spent years researching, reflecting, and analyzing how to best structure my block. It seemed every teacher in upper elementary was doing something a little bit different. Some were using *The Daily 5*, some were incorporating centers, and some taught the whole group and had the famous DEAR (Drop Everything and Read) time. It was also evident that not all teachers had the same time in their classrooms. That year, I had about 1 hour and 20 minutes a day to teach reading, writing, word study, and grammar, while others had a whopping 2 hours! While I may have loved the setup that the 2-hour-time-block teacher had, it just didn't work for what *I* needed.

Over the course of two years, I transitioned from a fourth-grade teacher to a multiage teacher, teaching grades four, five, and six. I was passionate about literacy instruction, and I worked tirelessly to find a solution to all my problems. Like many teachers, I struggled with my time and how to fit it all in. It seemed that I could never find the balance between the length of my lessons and how much work to assign my students. I'll be honest with y'all, I am a bit of a chatterbox. I was able to find a rhythm with my reading lessons at a certain point, but that meant that I still needed to find time to teach grammar, word study, and writing. It was a constant balancing act and any shift could throw off my routine, leaving me feeling stressed and overwhelmed.

I also struggled with meeting all the needs of the ranges of learners in my classroom. Despite being a fourth-through-sixth-grade teacher, I had students from a second-grade reading level all the way to a seventh-grade level in my classroom. *What do you do with that?* I lived in small groups, and at one point I was planning at least six different small groups for a single day. That's six different lessons, books, activities, organizers, and independent activities for each instructional day; it was absolutely exhausting. Trying to keep up with the varying readers was not sustainable. This is how teachers burn out and lose the love of teaching.

Finally, I struggled with developing a meaningful connection to what we were learning and how it related to the outside world. For me, learning has always been about understanding how things relate to me, my life, and my experiences. If I cannot make a connection, then what's the point? In order to have kids care about and see the value of what they are doing, we have to go beyond the worksheet. Trying to make learning meaningful and tap into each kids' interest sounds great, but how attainable is that when you have two blocks of 25 students?

While there were more struggles that I went through as an upper elementary teacher, those were the ones that weighed on me the most. I felt like a good teacher; I had the passion, and I knew the importance of brain-based strategies for how students learn. What I needed more than anything was a structure. Someone to help me understand how to put all the moving pieces in place so that they worked together in harmony. This is where we begin. I want to take you on the journey that I went through to find my ideal literacy block in upper elementary. In this book, I share the strategies and structures, and I offer example lessons and resources to help you find your own perfect rhythm. More than anything, I want to be that resource that I so desperately searched for years ago.

How to Use This Book

This book is divided into three key parts. Each part is developed in such a way that it will help guide you at various points in the school year. In the beginning, I encourage you to read through each part in order. They all build on each other and it is helpful to have the information in the right order, but this is not meant to be a one-time read. My goal with this book is to create a resource that will help motivate, re-inspire and align you to your goals throughout your career. Think of this as a tune-up for your car. You can do the basics – fill up the tank and get a wash – but occasionally, you need to get a tune-up. Being a teacher means that we have multiple things happening around us at one time. It can be easy to lose sight of what we should be doing and find things that seem easier. This book will always be here to help give you the kick in the butt you need to set things back right.

Part 1: The Basics

In this section of the book, I offer the necessary components to build the foundation for your literacy block. Everything in life consists of basic building blocks. These building blocks give you the ability to embellish and reflect your own personality and lifestyle, but the basic pieces are all the same. Think of an architect designing a building. Every building will have the same basic components: a foundation, walls, roof, windows, doors. You cannot have one without the other, and in the case of reading, you have to create a foundation that will hold up your routines and procedures all year and give students the opportunity for rigorous and authentic learning.

This section is perfect for new upper elementary teachers or for veteran teachers who needs a little refresher on setting up their literacy block. You can use this section at the beginning of each year to plan and remind yourself of the basic components for structuring your ideal literacy block. We often start the year expecting our students to behave, think, and understand the expectations that we ended with the previous school year. You will have to spend a lot of time molding and shaping these students into what you expect. You can also use this section mid-year, preferably in January, to re-establish the expectations and give you a little boost to the end of the school year.

You will find example schedules for a variety of timeframes, ideas for what to incorporate into your literacy block, lesson plan samples for establishing your block at the beginning of the school year, and how to establish student independence. Without these pieces to the puzzle, you may very well be stressed, overworked, and at a complete loss for how to teach your content.

Part 2: The Strategies

This is the fun section of the book! Once you've laid the foundation of your literacy block, you can now start thinking about how to create authentic, engaging, and rigorous lessons for your students. This is where the magic happens. It is important to note that this is not an exhaustive resource, but more so what I have found to be the most essential components for giving good instruction. Here, you can customize your literacy block and make it more appealing. This is when you get to add your creative twist so that it stands out.

As you read this section, think about your students, your school environment, and your own teaching style. Find ways to take these ideas and implement them in ways that work for you. This is meant to be your hub for activities, strategies, and ideas for planning your lessons. Use this section when you need to know where to go and how to teach something, or even as a refresher to authentic strategies that you can use again. I can assure you these are all winners in my classroom. This section is also helpful when you are in a rut and need a little bit of inspiration. Even as a veteran teacher, I have times when I simply go through the motions of everyday life. This section will inspire and motivate you to get back to that feeling you had at the beginning of the year.

You will find the structures for creating a killer mini-lesson with example lessons for multiple grade levels, and my methods for fitting it all in during 1 hour and 10 minutes. You'll also find a list of ideas for engaging your students in the lesson in order to create a student-centered classroom, and how to incorporate individual conferences when you have little time or processes.

Part 3: The More

In this section, you will find the parts that go beyond learning and create a passion for reading and writing. This is the extension of all your hard work, and it builds connections and experiences for your students that are meaningful. Going back to our architect, this is when the building is complete, and you can make it your own. This is the personalization and connection that happens. You have the sign that goes up on the outside of the building, the pictures that fill the hallways, and the names outside of the door. This is what you will use to extend and develop connections that will ultimately lead to students becoming lifelong readers.

You can use this section throughout the year to establish some of those critical elements that make reading authentic and relatable, but more importantly it makes learning attainable for all your students. During this stage, students are defining what they specifically need and how they will grow individually. This is when you create a learning environment that is personalized to their needs instead of that one-size-fits-all classroom.

You'll learn about practical and realistic methods for customizing a learning environment as well as ideas for helping students at any stage in their learning. You'll also learn some simple strategies for holding your students accountable for independent reading without it feeling too daunting. Finally, you will find the key to connecting all the learning back together through the power of read aloud.

This book will hopefully inspire you to develop a literacy workshop that goes beyond the isolated content areas and view reading and writing as one component that is embedded in everything we do. As you read, take time to reflect on your own practices and the areas that you want to change or revamp. As we go along this journey together, my hope is that you will find a joy for teaching literacy that doesn't consume your time and life outside of the classroom.

PART

I | The Basics

When I first started teaching kindergarten, we followed the first 20 days to build our reading and writing workshop. The plans were developed by my school district at the time, and they revolved around establishing the Daily 5 in our classrooms. Each day of the first 20 days had a specific part of the Daily 5 that we would introduce, and we would model and practice each part until we had a full workshop up and running. Seems great, right? It was scaffolded, and it gave teachers time to get to know the students and really establish those expectations from the very beginning.

The problem was that, as a young teacher, I found it repetitive. There was one component that I could never really wrap my brain around (until later in my career). Each day we had a Student of the Day. This student was celebrated and brought in a bag of items that represented them. They brought pictures for our bulletin board and a little page that described them. It was cute, in the beginning. Until you were celebrating a student every school day for the first 25 days. As a teacher, I was ready to jump into content, but the Student of the Day routine took up a lot of time. By day 10, I had an itch to start pulling groups, get into reading, and jump into the learning that I knew so many of my students needed.

I was impatient. I knew the expectations. I knew what the class was supposed to look and sound like, but it took time for me to learn that the classroom is not about *me*. The classroom, the lessons, the learning that was going to take place was (and still is) about my students. While they felt redundant and way too long, the days spent reviewing the expectations were the foundation of our entire year. Without the foundation of your literacy block, your students will unravel and soon forget the expectations. This is usually the time when you start to pull out your hair because you feel as though you've talked about it enough and you can't understand why your students are not understanding the lesson.

Building the foundation for your literacy block is like building your wardrobe. I love clothes, but my wardrobe is pretty boring. When I was younger, my mother and I used to watch "What Not to Wear" with Stacey London and Clinton Kelly. I loved them! What we learned from them was to start with basics and build your wardrobe from there. These included a nice white shirt, a good pair of jeans, a button-down shirt, and more. These *basics* were the pieces that you could always fall back on if something just wasn't feeling right. As an adult, I have taken this concept of basics and gone a little overboard. Everything in my closet can be classified as a *basic* form of clothing. I stick to neutral colors such as black, white, beige, and browns. I've managed to take all the guesswork out of what I have to wear.

Creating a wardrobe solely around the basics gives me the option to mix and match any bottom to any top. I can decide to hop on to any of the trending fashion trains to spice up my life, but my basics are always there. I have something to fall back on during the times when I don't feel like wearing anything else. My basics are my comfort zone. I can always rely on them because they are classic. Having these basics allow me to focus on the things that are more important.

This idea of taking all the guesswork out of your literacy block is what you are trying to aim for in Part 1 of this book. The goal is to create a comfort zone for you and your students. The work that you put into your block in the very beginning stages might seem boring (just like my wardrobe), but it's necessary for incorporating other elements later down the road. This is the lesson I wish I had known when I first started teaching. Instead of rolling my eyes at doing another day of painstakingly boring tasks, I wish I had been excited about these early moments. Without them, the fun moments could never have happened.

Think for a moment about your classroom or the classroom that you plan on having in the future. What do you want it to feel like? Most every teacher would want their classroom to feel welcoming and fun. Having a classroom that makes learning fun will help your students feel excited about learning. However, if you've ever been to a birthday party, sleepover, or any form of children's event that is classified as fun, then you've probably experienced the chaos. As a teacher attending these events, I've felt the deep desire to do a quick *CLASS, CLASS* chant or a simple clapping routine to gain control.

Creating a fun classroom has its appeal but it also comes with disadvantages. Fun causes opportunities for disarray, lack of control, and inconsistencies. I am not trying to tell you to never have fun in your classroom. I love fun! In fact, I have had my fair share of times when we've completely dropped what we were doing to mix in a little bit of excitement. For instance, I once held a pirate day with a partner fourth-grade teacher. Students were placed in teams, and they had to get their ship to the stolen treasure. Each challenge focused on a reading or math concept that had been taught. I also had a Minecraft day that served as a fun way to teach difficult (and otherwise boring) reading and math concepts. Students each got their own Steve Head, and each activity incorporated elements from the game. I've held murder mysteries and escape rooms just to break up the daily mundane tasks in our classroom. However, we always had our foundation to fall back on when things got a little crazy. Even after crazy days due to schedule changes or a more engaging lesson, students always knew the expectations and could follow them without much assistance the next day. I knew that the day after having *fun* would run perfectly smoothly because we had worked so hard to establish these expectations from the very beginning. Having a deep-rooted foundation to your literacy block is your goal to feeling successful.

Creating this foundation will set the stage for what and how your students will engage in reading and writing throughout the year. In the following chapters, we explore the necessary components for establishing an authentic literacy workshop. As you read through these chapters, take time and reflect on your current practices and how you can modify them to fit the points in each chapter. The purpose of this book is not to mimic me as a teacher, but rather to help you identify what works best for you, your classroom, and your students.

1 | No Time for That

As I continued to grow as a teacher during my first three years in the profession, I stuck to the philosophy "*Go Big or Go Home.*" Seeing how I was a Texan, born and raised, it was only fitting. However, as a teacher, this is not always the best philosophy. During my third year of teaching kindergarten in Alabama, I learned this lesson in a big way. I learned that sometimes the big work we put into things does not always give us the reward we are looking for. In this case, it wasn't serving all my students, and it certainly was not serving me.

We all go through professional development that gets us thinking about how we can do things differently for our students. Some of the professional development that I participated in revolved around differentiating instruction in order to serve your students' individual needs. Seemed easy enough. You make a little change here, do something slightly different for another, and now you're differentiating! This idea took me down a rabbit hole. I pulled small groups in kindergarten, as do many teachers. I had five different groups that I would meet with regularly.

Each of the groups were assigned a color: red, yellow, green, orange, and blue. As time continued with these groups, I began to contemplate whether I could differentiate their independent time at their Daily 5 stations. At the time, I had specific bins that contained word work stations that *all* students would choose from. This posed some challenges because Student A may have needed additional letter practice and Student B needed more focused digraph practice. I devised a plan to customize the word work stations to the color of the groups, but it didn't stop there! I then took each group and broke them into three categories: popcorn words, word families, and CVC words.

This meant that in order to keep my students engaged, I was planning out at least one new station for each bin. This totaled 15 new activities each week. Now, yes, I was able to take a lot of what we practiced in our small groups and place them into their word work bins, but I was still doing the work of creating stations. I had also placed additional pressure on myself to have themed activities that revolved around what we were learning in science and social studies. This only increased the amount of work and time that I was putting into creating resources for one small timeframe of my teaching day.

Did my students even notice the themed lessons? Was it benefiting them in any way? It took a few years to realize that the effort that I was putting in as a teacher was not impacting their learning in the most effective way. So why did I spend so much time creating these resources? How much of what we are creating and planning really benefit our students?

Before I started teaching, I had various jobs. I worked in retail, then became a waitress with a quick promotion to culinary manager. I worked as a teller in a bank and as a receptionist at a veterinary clinic. My time working in these various positions taught me a lot about input and output. The input is the work that you put into the position that you hold within the company, and the output is the reward or benefit that is reaped due to the input. Many within the business or productivity realm reference the 80/20 rule in determining where and on what you should be spending most of your time. The idea is that 20% of your efforts will give you 80% of your results.

I took this theory of productivity and began applying it to education. I wanted to find the 20% that was truly giving me the biggest impact when it came to my instructional and productivity practices. The more I worked to understand this principle the more I realized the importance of focusing on the 20% of my lesson activities that will give my students' the greatest impact. In other words, there were certain components of my lesson that would help my students understand the concept far more than other parts. Take a simple lesson on informational text structures. During a 60-minute time block, I might have a warm-up, mini-lesson, partner practice, independent practice, and stations or independent reading. Which do you think would offer the greatest impact? Depending on how long I spend on each component that day, the mini-lesson and partner practice might give me the greatest reward. So why spend so much time on areas of our teaching that just don't help our kids move forward in their learning?

Parts of Your Literacy Block

Your literacy block will have many moving parts. Each of these parts should work in conjunction with one another to create a flow that makes sense and supports the learning of your students. As you read through the options for building your literacy block, keep in mind the timeframe and your own teaching style. You always have room to tweak items and make them work for you and your students. You will also notice that I stay away from including *centers* in the upper elementary classroom. Literacy centers take up too much time and give little to no flexibility to meeting the needs in the classroom. These centers discourage students from being independent by dictating exactly what students should be working on during each rotation. The goal of every upper elementary classroom is to help guide students to make choices based on the learning that fits them best. Many of the following options will help give you ideas of how to structure your block and build independence with your students.

Warm-Up Activity

A warm-up activity is a quick, 5- to 10-minute review of a previous skill that will help warm up their brains for the lesson that day. It is meant to help focus them on the topic that you are discussing and give them an opportunity to switch their thinking. This is especially helpful if they are transitioning from a different subject or coming in right after lunch and recess.

Many teachers will use this time to do a spiral review or what some call "bell ringers." While these may seem easy and beneficial for teachers to use, the problem is that many of these premade spiral practices do not align with the focus lesson of the day. If you have students complete a question on characters for their review but the content lesson consists of informational text structures, how does this benefit them? Instead, help create connections and meaning to your warm-up activities. Think of specific content areas connected to your instruction. For example, if you are teaching the parts of plot, you may want to quickly review the types of conflict or questions related to the characters of the story you read. This process will allow students to start thinking about the content that you are going to introduce during your lesson.

In order to make this manageable and meaningful for you and your students, think about the delivery of your warm-up activity. Are you going to have the questions premade and printed at their desk, or bound into a book? Will it be projected on your smartboard or projection screen, and will you have students complete it in their journals? Or will you have a foldable component to make the activity more interactive? Whatever you choose, think about this one question: *What is your purpose?* So often we give students extensive tasks that take away from learning. Foldables are a great example of this! While they increase engagement, make things look pretty, and allow students to effectively organize information, the cutting and gluing take away from the focus of working and discussing the content.

To give you a better idea of how this looks in my classroom, I post my question or questions on my projector using my iPad. Students come in, take a seat, and read the board. Each day the focus can look a little different. Here are some ideas to help get you started:

- Post a task card or set of cards that students complete on a whiteboard and then discuss.
- Have a short passage in which students read and then organize information in their journals. For example, completing a compare-and-contrast of the content.

- Post a sentence that students can diagram.

- Have a series of problems for students to practice a grammar skill: subject/predicate, compound-complex, and so on.

- Have a journal prompt that will encourage them to brainstorm topics or write a poem.

The possibilities are endless when it comes to creating a warm-up activity that will suit the needs of your classroom. As students work on the activity, this is a time to circle about the classroom and get an idea of how they are meeting expectations. This will give you an idea of what you will have to reteach or which kids to pull for additional practice. Review the question or questions by holding a discussion with the class. Don't go too overboard with the number of questions! You want to remember that this is not your lesson but rather a quick introduction. Keep the practice quick and the feedback short. You can even take notes of students whom you can pull for small groups to review the concept in more detail. When you are finished, students will easily transition to the next part of the class period.

Open Meeting

Think of an open meeting as a pep talk. At the start of any game, a coach will gather the players and give a quick pep talk to ensure everyone knows the strategy and are inspired and motivated to go out and do their very best. This is exactly the purpose of having a 5- to 10-minute open meeting at the start of each class. If you meet with more than one cohort of classes then this is a great time to greet everyone, discuss what they are working on for the day, and give students an opportunity to share and discuss books they have been reading.

Beginning with an open meeting helps to build a classroom community, and I think it is essential to ensure that every part of my literacy block runs smoothly. If you have the space available in your classroom, I suggest having students sit in a circle on the floor or bring their chairs to the meeting area. I have also invested a little bit of money into having a collection of stools to make it easy to create a circle with sixth-grade bodies. The reason for the circle is so that all students can see one another and hold a conversation easily. Once you are all seated, you can begin by greeting students and setting the expectations for the day. Here are some helpful ideas of what you can share during this time:

- Learning targets or objectives for the day.
- Whom you will be meeting with for individual conferences.
- Which small or flexible groups you will be meeting with.
- Assignments that are due, or independent tasks that need to be completed by the end of class.
- New books to the classroom library or student book recommendations (this is a great time to include book talks, but I will share more on that in Chapter 8).

Remember that this meeting is meant to be short. Try to avoid rambling, and have a specific agenda. All the preceding suggestions listed do not need to happen every day, especially if you have a central location with this information displayed. It can be helpful to reference the display to encourage students to use the information. It is important to model how to use reference material if you expect students to use it themselves. At the end of your open meeting, you can then dismiss students or get started with your mini-lesson.

Reading Mini-Lesson

The reading mini-lesson is the heart of your literacy block, and it can be the most challenging piece to master as a teacher. After more than a decade of teaching, I still find myself learning how to improve my skills to craft an efficient mini-lesson. This time of your literacy block should last anywhere between 12 to 20 minutes, and the purpose is to model the skill that students will be practicing during their independent reading time. Even in the upper elementary classroom, the mini-lesson sets the stage for students to understand the content.

During your lesson, you can choose to either have students at their seats or continue to stay seated in a circle. I find that some of my classes are more focused when seated in a circle and others would rather sit in their seats. Experiment with what works best for your class and know that this may look different from other years. Your mini-lesson will be focused on your learning target or objective. Creating a flow to your lessons is important as students will become comfortable with how you teach your lessons and they can focus more on the learning rather than the format.

When structuring your lesson, think about how you can scaffold the strategy. Since the lesson is only 12–20 minutes, you will have to be very strategic and planned so that you don't fall behind. Here are some helpful tips to keep in mind as you begin planning out your lessons:

- Prepare all your materials in advance.
- Begin by modeling your thinking to students through a text you have previously read with them.
- Include a shared reading to get students thinking about how they would implement the strategy or skill. In this strategy, teachers invite students to help with the reading process as a method for scaffolding. It offers a gradual release of work so that students do not become overwhelmed and have an opportunity to build confidence.
- Create space for students to practice in pairs after you model the strategy or skill. Try to minimize movement as it will increase the time of your lesson.
- Provide immediate feedback to students to clear up any misconceptions.

As you continue to develop your own style for teaching, you will find some engaging practices to fall back on. In Chapters 4 and 5, you will find strategies and activities to help you to craft your mini-lessons. Be prepared with copies of pages from books, sentence stems, and any other activities for students to keep the lesson moving quickly and to limit students from getting distracted.

Independent Practice

It's important to give your students time to practice what you modeled during the mini-lesson. This time can look a little different each day, but the goal is always the same: to engage in authentic and meaningful discussions around reading. How you choose to structure this time may fluctuate during various points in the year. At the beginning of any school year, you might have students work more independently. As the year progresses and they learn the expectations of the classroom, you can begin to incorporate more opportunities for partner and group work.

The activities will also vary in the amount of time it takes for students to complete. As you may have guessed, the time will generally increase as students become more familiar with your expectations and as you increase in the difficulties of skills and strategies. Crafting the right type of practice will be like the scene from *The Three Little Bears*; you will have to find the "just right" spot to keep your students from losing focus or getting frustrated.

As you plan the practice portion of your lesson, focus on how you want your students to demonstrate their understanding. Do you have to take it as a grade? Do your students need to write out their responses in a paragraph? Try and keep the practice short, concise, and authentic. Here are some suggestions of independent practice that I have done in my own classroom:

- Have students respond to an open-ended question in their journal or a discussion board.
- Give students an exit ticket to complete on the learning topic.
- Have students complete a graphic organizer.
- Give students a means for organizing information from a text (e.g., using text structures).

On the topic of grading: not everything has to be graded, but it is important to give feedback. One area that many teachers struggle with is getting

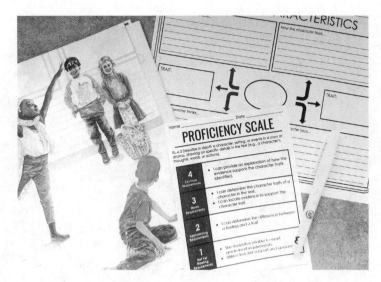

Figure 1.1 Rubric aligned with learning target.

students to take ownership of their learning. One way of encouraging this is to give feedback as often as possible. To do this create a rubric for each learning target that you teach. For instance, in one week I may teach identifying the main idea of an informational text with key supporting details. I can create a standard rubric that assesses this learning target and that creates the space to give students feedback (see Figure 1.1).

Independent Reading

Every teacher can tell you about the importance of independent reading. In fact, many administrators are pushing for teachers to incorporate DEAR time in classrooms. We all know the impact that reading has on a student's learning, and independent reading is a time for students to engage with books, explore new lands, have discussions, and expand on their sense of the world around them. However, having a time in which everyone reads at the same time each day, as DEAR suggests, does more harm than good. When students feel as though it is a chore or a to-do item, they are less likely to develop their own intrinsic passion for reading. Here are some items to consider when students engage in independent reading:

Figure 1.2 Book display of Book Challenge.

- Create a 20/30/40 Book Challenge (see Figure 1.2). This strategy, introduced by Donalyn Miller in her book *The Book Whisperer*, challenges students to read a variety of books from various genres. As students meet certain goals these milestones can be celebrated with the class.

- Have students keep track of the books they read using a classroom display. I use a curtain hook for students to keep their book names, an idea inspired by Jill Shafer from Hello Fifth. In simple terms, this is a visual in your classroom that students can add to in order to show what books or how many books they have read. You can be simple or more creative by attaching this to the theme of your classroom.

- Have students keep a log of the books they read but not the number of pages they read each day. Avoid using a daily reading log. These, especially when you have a short literacy block, can be challenging for students to maintain.

- Refrain from using a response journal. Again, these can be challenging to maintain, and are hard to provide feedback to learners. Instead, ask yourself whether students need to respond in a written format or if they can share during the closing circle time at the end of class. You can also have students respond through a class blog, discussion posts, or other formats that will engage and offer a more collaborative form of communication.

- Once a week or every other week, have students respond to the books they are reading in a discussion post or journal. Do these on a day when you need to *catch up* or want to hold more conferences versus teaching a new lesson.

- Get students to hold book talks once a month. This is discussed in Chapter 8 and gets your students sharing what they've read with their peers!

The Writing Mini-Lesson

The writing mini-lesson is much like the reading mini-lesson. It should be short and concise to the learning target that you would like your students to demonstrate. The most important part of crafting a writing mini-lesson is to ensure that you are modeling *how* to write in front of your students. Writing is one of, if not the most, challenging components taught in schools. Oftentimes it is placed in importance behind reading. I'd argue that writing should be leading the fight because it is the higher-level thinking skill needed to analyze, observe, and discuss during our reading time. Instead of separating your reading and writing block into two isolated times, consider calling your entire block a literacy block as it offers more flexibility versus pinning you in a corner. The more we can create an equal respect and relationship between reading and writing, the more our students will grow in all areas.

Now, modeling how to write in front of students can be challenging because many teachers will wait to brainstorm, write, and revise in front of students. This can take what should be a quick lesson into a lesson that lasts the entire class period. Have a clear focus. Break your lesson into the various components of the writing process. One day you can model how to brainstorm, the next day model how to outline and so forth. The trick to this is that all your writing is already done in advance. What you model should not be thoroughly authentic because it will take time and delay the process of getting through your mini-lesson. Instead, have a sketch of what you want to target during your mini-lesson on paper. This will keep the lesson quick and snappy while also getting the point across.

As with everything else that we have discussed so far, you will find your own style for teaching your writing lesson. The important factors are to have a larger goal. Ask yourself: *What do I want my students to complete today?* This will serve as a guide as you create your lessons. Here are some other items to think about as you plan:

- Connect your reading and writing standards. This will allow you to quickly reference authors you are reading and strategies you have been analyzing during your reading block.

- When writing your outline, have some sentences prewritten and discuss the process that you took to write them. From there you can model writing a few more sentences and even get your students involved when helping to word the sentences properly.

- Have your writing already done! Having your example writing completed before you start the new unit will ensure that you are fully prepared. This will be your North Star as you craft your lessons.

Another important element to include in your writing mini-lesson is an opportunity for students to constantly revise their writing. When we think about the writing process, we often see it posted in a linear fashion. Writing is not linear. In fact, the revision stage happens at all points in the writing process. Students should have opportunities to revise their brainstorms, organizers, outlines, and rough drafts. The more they revise, the more they understand, and the easier it will be to write their stories.

Independent Writing/Practice

How often have you looked out to see a handful of students staring at a blank page? Independent writing is hard, and it can be even more challenging to be there for all your students at one time. The secret of this timeframe is not to give your students immense freedom with their writing, but to help guide them through the process. If you have created a mini-lesson that is focused and has a clear objective, students will be more likely to succeed when working independently. Therefore it is crucial to break your lessons into small, tangible, and understandable parts.

The practice that your students are completing during this time should mirror the lesson that you modeled earlier. So, if you modeled how to brainstorm a character of your writing then students should complete that same exact organizer.

> **Quick Tip:** Use the same organizers that you use in your reading class. This will limit the confusion over *how* to use the organizer and have students focus more on the content itself. However, one big question asked among teachers is what should students do when they are finished with their writing? In Chapter 2, I share how to establish your blocks so that students know exactly what to do when they are done, but here is a list of ideas that you can have readily available for students to practice their writing.

- Provide comic book paper for students to create stories. This is a fun and easy way for students to get more comfortable with sharing small stories.
- Offer fun writing prompts. Now, I am *not* a fan of prompt writing but there is something to be said about having students write to a prompt effectively. Have these available, but I would not force all students to use them.

Figure 1.3 Author station.

- Incorporate technology when possible. Apps such as Book Creator, Google Slides, and more can offer another element of engagement when it comes to writing.

- Create areas in your classroom that focus on specific goals. We will get into this a little more in Chapter 7 on how to set these up.

- Establish an author station for students to mimic (see Figure 1.3). There is no better way to develop your own style of writing than by looking at those you admire the most. Rotate authors that you want students to mimic. You could have the book *Saturdays and Teacakes* by Lester Laminack, and have students use repetition on something that was a tradition for him when he was younger. Rotate these out frequently to inspire students to write.

- Decide in advance where you would like them to complete their writing assignments. Will you have a folder to maintain organizers and writing samples or maybe a binder?

No matter the organizational type, use these consistently so that it takes the guesswork out for your students. This can also include writing materials. Having a station located in your classroom with topic ideas and a variety of writing utensils can engage students in writing their own stories.

Grammar Practice/Word Work

Do you feel like grammar and word work only get taken down from the top shelf, dusted off, and taught from time to time? If you are someone who has a tight schedule, you may very well feel this way. Grammar and word work are key components that are often forgotten or used as a time-filler or to grab a score to report at the end of the nine-week period. One way that I have found to be beneficial and easy for incorporating grammar and word work is to utilize a mentor sentence of the week. Each week, take your mentor text that you are using for your reading or writing lessons. Think about a focus such as subject/predicate, complex sentences, dialogue, and so on, and find a sentence that will allow students to explore the concept you have chosen.

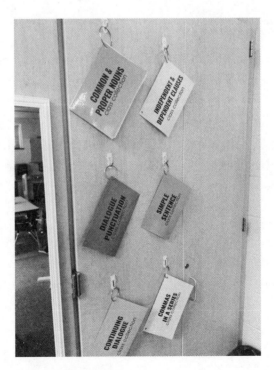

Figure 1.4 Classroom collections.

Once you've taught the concept through a mentor text, students need to have opportunities to interact and regularly engage in the grammar concepts and words. However, finding ways to incorporate these into your schedule can be challenging. In Chapter 7, we dive into setting goals and having dedicated stations established in your classroom to support students in their goals. Here are a few ways that can assist you in maintaining this practice regularly:

- Have a bin of premade activities that will allow your students to practice. You can use games such as War, Spoons, I Have/Who Has, Go Fish and more that allow you to take the rules of the game and create fun, competitive practice games.

- Have a section for task cards for students to complete as part of a lesson or goal practice.

- Use classroom collections, an idea from Jeff Anderson's book *Patterns of Power*, to encourage students to find specific concepts in their readings and share it with the class (see Figure 1.4).

Closing Meeting

At the end of each class, hold a 3- to 5-minute meeting where you can review the objective of the day. I suggest holding this meeting the same way in which you start the class time, gathered in a circle where every student feels a part of the community. The closing meeting can be easy to forget but it can be one of the most valuable components of your literacy block. This is a time to add the finishing touches and tie the bow on the day. Use this time to not only review what happened during class, but to celebrate each other. This is a great time to highlight students and share the great things you observed in class. Here are some other things you can celebrate during this time:

- Goals that were met by individual students.

- Students who have finished reading a book.

- Students who set an example during independent time.

- Students who used strategies you taught.

Even if you are strapped for time and cannot get your class in a circle, take a couple of minutes to create an ending to the class time while students are seated at their desks. This might look different on busy days, but defining the ending will help your students transition, and it can contribute to building a classroom community.

How to Fit It All In

The flow that you create for your literacy block will depend on the time available for you and your students. This can vary from class to class and year to year. After reading the list of possibilities you may think one of two things: (1) *Seems easy enough to fit it all in* or (2) *I don't have the time to get all this into my literacy block.* I completely understand. There have been years where I had 90 minutes of literacy time, and other years in which I only had 60 minutes. Crafting your literacy block is all about your strategy to use the time effectively.

The goal of any literacy block is for all students to work on their tasks, meet goals, and collaborate with peers, while you meet with groups or individual students. We have all dreamed of what our blocks could possibly look like, but the reality is that things emerge; we will have situations that need our attention, and it may feel like you are missing some of the literacy components. Whatever the case, the pieces that were previously shared will help to guide you in crafting a logical flow that works.

But what about those of you who can't fit in both the reading and writing lesson? I have a solution for you! Integration will give back time in your literacy block, and it will help you in creating a deeper connection with your students. The only downside is that it will require you to think more strategically about what you teach and when you teach it. In order to do this, you will have some days in which you teach a reading lesson and other days in which you teach a writing lesson. It may seem disjointed, but the content that you teach is what will connect the days. For example, you might discuss the setting of a story and how an author develops this in their writing. As the week progresses you might transition to having students brainstorm and develop the setting of their own writing, and you may add a lesson on using adjectives to create show-versus-tell sentences. Each of the lessons connect to create a seamless flow from one day to the next. If you would like to continue learning how to create these lessons, you can visit www.buildingtheliteracyblockresources.com to download the free resource that breaks down the writing units and the reading standards that match the topic.

As you construct your literacy block, begin with what you need to have first and build from there. For example, you know that you need to have a mini-lesson, independent practice, and (I highly suggest) an open and closing meeting. Take the timeframes and subtract those from your total time block. Do you have time left? If yes, add the components that fit your teaching. If not, then incorporate integration that will allow you to hit all your standards. We talk more about this topic as we continue with the next chapters.

No matter the time you have for your literacy block, it cannot be successful without routines. As painful as it might seem, think about every possible movement that is going to occur in your classroom. The more you can visualize what the day is going to look and sound like, the more you are able to be proactive and ensure the day runs smoothly. Take some time to sit down and think through routines that you want to build with your students. It can be helpful to have an ever-growing document either in a notebook or inside of a Google Doc. Here are some questions to consider to help spark routines:

- How will students go to their desks?
- How do you plan on grabbing their attention?
- Where will students place their belongings when instruction begins?
- How will students grab materials from the room (e.g., writing folders, notebooks, etc.)?
- When will students go to the library to check out new books?

- How will you notify students that they are going to meet you for small groups or individual conferences?
- What will students do when they are finished with assignments?
- How will students leave your classroom?

Chapter Wrap-Up

Structuring your block is the most important part of building a strong foundation in your classroom. The more detailed you are with visualizing every minute of the day, the easier it will be to manage behaviors and create an optimum learning environment. When you can design a space in which every component of your block is purposeful, you will feel confident planning your lessons. It will create a seamless flow for your students, and they will know exactly what to expect. After reading this chapter, consider the following steps on getting started with successfully building independent learners:

- Take time to identify the requirements that are set forth by your district or school, and then work to build the remainder of components of your block.
- Take into consideration the length of your block. To have an idea of how each component will fit, assign each component a max timeframe and see if it adds up to your schedule.
- If you are struggling on time, and need to fit in more literacy block components, then decide on whether you will be conducting A/B days or have alternating consecutive days of reading and writing.

2 | We Built This City

Did you ever get nervous the night before the start of school (see Figure 2.1)? Did you worry about whether people would like you, if you would remember where to go, and if you'd have a chance to go to the bathroom during the day? If you're thinking that I'm talking about a time when you were a kid, you're wrong. Well, you are kind of wrong; I'm sure that we have all felt this way at some point or another, but I'm referencing the first day of school as a teacher. Even after years of teaching, the first day of school is still hard. My nerves are at an all-time high; I have high expectations for myself, and more importantly, I worry about whether students will be happy with their new classroom.

I remember some of my first days of school as a student, and it was spent at my desk looking over the syllabus and reading the student handbook. It was boring, and it left very little to look forward to that year. I did not want to be that teacher. I wanted to help students see that learning could be fun. Getting students excited about coming to school and creating an inviting and inclusive environment was always my focus. First impressions matter, and I wanted to give my students a day that would set the tone for the entire school year. This required paying attention to every detail of the day. It needed to be perfect, and I wanted it to be action-packed, filled with fun activities, games, and lots of smiles. However, this idea of making every minute fun was not attainable. I needed to talk about procedures and routines. I needed to show them what school could look like in multiple facets. The reality is that every day cannot be a party. I learned that I needed to find a way to balance the mundane with flair and fun.

25

Figure 2.1 Beginning of the year.

How can we create that balance for ourselves and our students? My students can still have fun while also setting expectations at the start of the year. Now, the way in which I structure the first day of school is very intentional. There is a balance when creating plans for introducing students to their classroom for the year. To give you a bigger picture, my first day of school comprises these components:

Welcome students. Make every student feel welcomed and recognized on the first day by standing by the front door. I like to take this opportunity to stand outside of my classroom, introduce myself, learn their name, show them where the bathroom is located, and then show them their seat in the classroom. If you are like me and you have a homeroom class, I have students take their backpacks and place them on their seats. There is always time to model how to put their things away. This limits questions in the beginning and helps to allay some of their nervousness.

Welcome activity. Find something simple for students to do at their seats while you are still greeting other students. Stay away from anything that includes too much reading or writing as some students may struggle with this activity, and it can feel frustrating to have it on the first day of school. I enjoy having a word search with the names of their classmates, a simple coloring page, and some picture books placed in a basket at the center of the table for students to look through. Having options will ensure those early finishers have something to do without interrupting you while you say hello to all your students.

Morning meeting. Right after announcements, lunch counts, and attendance, hold a morning meeting. I shared a little about the idea of a morning meeting back in Chapter 1. You can hold it while students are at their seats, but there is something special about bringing your class to a meeting area. During the morning meeting, greet everyone again and allow students to greet one another; share their answers to a question of the day, and engage in an activity. You can find tons of resources on holding morning meetings online, but a great place to start is at the source: Responsive Classroom. There you will find out more information about the process of holding a morning meeting and ideas for greets, shares, and activities.

Simple/Basic routines. It's inevitable that you spend some time focusing on routines and procedures. You have to do it, but you have more control over which routines you choose to focus on. Remember, ease students into the school year; too much, too soon is only going to confuse and overwhelm students. On the first day of school, I like to think about the most important routines needed to get through the day. It always feels like you will get a lot accomplished, but the reality is that everything moves at a snail's pace (except for time). Make sure you review how to line up, how to go to the bathroom, how to put away their backpacks and items they bring, what to do at recess and how to give their full attention. Everything else can wait.

Get-to-know-you activity. There is nothing more exciting than getting to know your students on the first day, but they are not all ready to start spilling their life story. Give them a small informational page that they can complete. I do a variety of these each year. One year it was a basic question and answer, other years it was a newsletter style info page, and most recently, I had a more detailed page that had them decorate an outline of a person to look like them and fill in questions about themselves. If an activity requires cutting or gluing, consider preparing these in advance to limit time and confusion. Always think about the focus, and on that first day of school, it is never about pulling out loads of materials for them to work with. Your goal on the first day of school is to learn a little bit of information and allow students to ease into the school year.

Celebrate. We always have end-of-the-year celebrations, but what about the beginning of the year? If we celebrate when they leave us, then we should absolutely celebrate when they join us. I'm not talking about a full-blown party on the first day of school, but instead, how about setting aside 60–90 minutes for you to create a little bit of excitement? I love breakouts, escape rooms, and puzzles. They get kids talking, thinking, and working with one another to compete with the class. I've used a variety of beginning of the year breakouts to get my students in groups, working together, and solving the puzzles. As students break out, they are rewarded with a certificate and a small prize such as pop rocks, lollipops, and other treats. If some groups struggle with solving the puzzles, I always lend a helping hand to make sure they are on the right track. It's a great way to break the ice and get students excited about the school year.

Closing circle. There is nothing more rewarding than ending the day the same way it started. At the close of the day, seat students and have them share something they enjoyed about the day and a question they might still have. Now that they have spent time with you, they are more willing to open a conversation. Discuss what you all accomplished and give them an idea of what to expect the next day. You can incorporate activities that encourage sharing, but keep these ideas for later in the year when students have a solid understanding of your expectations.

Aligned with the idea of balance, you'll notice that my first day plan (see Figure 2.2) has both seated activities and some that incorporate movement for students. As you get started with planning out the first few weeks of

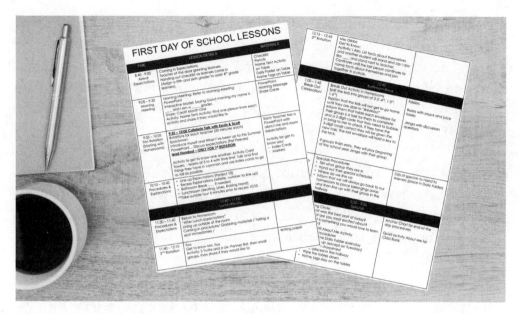

Figure 2.2 First day of school lesson plan.

school, try to weave fun activities and more mundane procedures so that you are constantly moving toward this larger goal of creating the ideal literacy block. However, once you get past that first day of school, the big question is: *Where do I go from here?* You certainly don't want to jump into your content lessons too early without setting expectations, nor do you want to take too long to jump into content.

Most schools will give you a specific timeframe for starting your content lessons, and this might mean starting on the second day of school! While this might not be ideal to build rapport with your students and establish routines, there are other methods, such as quick morning meeting activities that you can incorporate at other points in your day. Others have a little more leverage in determining when they can begin their lessons, and while they think it is best to *hit the ground running*, they will have challenges later on in the school year. This is all related to building independence, which we continue to explore in the next chapter. Here are a list of challenges that you or your students might face if you don't take the appropriate time to build your literacy block:

- **A lack of understanding procedures.** Students need multiple opportunities to practice procedures. This includes proper modeling, and giving feedback. Any teacher will tell you that the beginning-of-the-year procedures are time-consuming. If you jump into your curriculum too early, you are likely not taking the time to address the procedures with enough detail.

- **A dependency on your guidance.** Building independence is important, and like procedures, it takes time to develop. In order to create independent learners, you'll need to make them feel confident to make choices on their own, and create procedures and systems that your students are able to use.

- **A struggle to develop ownership and independence in their own learning.** The goal with every classroom is to develop lifelong learners. With the way that technology and society is changing, it is important to teach students how to learn rather than what they need to learn. Yes, we still have to teach the basics, but we need to be mindful to create thinkers in and outside of the classroom.

- **A structured or fixed classroom environment.** Curriculum too early in the year will require a lot of direction from the teacher. With little time spent on developing independence and procedures, students will look to you for what they should be doing next. This will make any changes to your daily routine overwhelming for you and your students.

While getting started with your content too soon can cause some challenges, starting your literacy block too late can also be detrimental. On the complete opposite end of the spectrum, there are many teachers who want to focus on getting to know kids before starting their literacy blocks. I am a big proponent of knowing your students and focusing on the whole child, but the reality is that kids need structure. Students thrive with routine, and while you do not have to dive into analyzing characters in the first month of school, it is helpful to teach students some of the basic skills that will help them be successful independently. The biggest concern with starting your block too late is creating the norm that every day is going to be an art or fun day. It's basically the equivalent to going over to Grandma's house knowing you can do whatever you want.

We need to find a middle ground where we are not *fluffing* our blocks with cute art projects to deck our hallways, but also not boring our kids with content, causing them to dread coming to school each day. Balance is the answer to it all, but unfortunately, I don't have the answer to how much you can have of each. To be honest, this will look different for many people. What works for my class may not work for yours, but I can tell you that taking the first month to get to know your students, while it may seem like caring, will lead to other issues. Here are some of the effects from starting your literacy block too late in the year:

- **Inconsistency with everyday routines.** Spending too much time on activities that don't help you create structure will leave your students guessing at what the block is going to bring. You'll find your students asking the dreaded question of *what are we doing today?* The purpose of your block is to model routines and procedures, but too much of it can cause students to feel bored and lose focus.

- **More work to develop beginning of the year lessons.** The beginning of the school year is already a draining process, and there is no need to drag it on longer than necessary. The longer you take to get into routine, the more lessons you will need to create that may or may not be relevant to your daily routine.

- **Lack of proper scaffolding.** The beginning of the year is often filled with fun get-to-know-you or classroom community activities. While these are incredibly essential to developing a community filled with accepting and growth mindset students, these activities in your literacy block will create a lack of consistency and scaffolding to creating routines. Embed these ideas of community by incorporating them into your lessons for developing your block versus creating separate activities. For example, teach students to respond to reading using your learning management system by reading a book like *The Memory String* by Eve Bunting. Have students make a connection and share a memory they have about someone they love. This keeps the focus on scaffolding the structure of your block while also learning more about one another.

- **Behavior concerns.** A lack of consistency and routines will cause students to struggle with focus during your lessons. You'll find students wondering what is happening next, and asking questions constantly about what they should be doing. Kids thrive in a structured environment, and creating a purposeful and engaging routine will limit the behaviors in your classroom.

Now let's look back at this idea of balance and how it can help to establish your ideal literacy block. How can you balance the need to get started with your content while also supporting and getting to know your students? The answer is never as simple as we would like it to be, but I can offer some ideas that have benefited me. The first is scaffolding the components that will eventually create your literacy block. This means scaffolding routines, procedures, and groups. The more you can scaffold the process, the more efficient and understanding your students will be when you are ready to begin running a full-blown workshop model.

How can scaffolding help you in creating your ideal block? To better understand the importance of scaffolding, think of this metaphor: a child does not learn to walk immediately. It takes months for a child to be able to lift their head, roll over, crawl, stand up, walk, and then run. It's a process. The process never changes, but the speed in which each child learns every component varies. One child might start walking at 11 months and another may not learn until the 14-month mark. Scaffolding is just that; it is a process. Once you identify your process, the steps needed to get to your ideal literacy block, the speed in which you take this process can change year-to-year depending on your class. The great thing is that if you take the time to plan out your process, it never changes and it makes planning your lessons a whole lot easier.

Not only does scaffolding benefit you, it also greatly benefits your students. The process that you develop makes learning the routines and procedures explicit for your students. They will have specific goals each day that will define exactly what they need to do for each of the moving parts during your literacy block. This will make learning and remembering the routines you teach more attainable. Think about a time when you attended a full day workshop. At the end of the day, you probably felt like your brain was going to explode with the amount of information you just had to consume. Your students experience this every day. Scaffolding your routines and expectations will help to gradually teach your learners without overloading them with information.

> **Quick Tip:** As you scaffold the routines and procedures of your literacy block, remember to review the previous day's lesson objectives. This will encourage students to continue working on old objectives while developing new ones. Use language such as: *Yesterday we . . . And today we are going to . . .*

How Many Days?

During my time teaching kindergarten, my school followed the first 20 days from the Daily 5. This meant that each day there was a specific lesson that I needed to teach to introduce an element of the Daily 5. As students got comfortable with the routine, another would be added and then by day 20, students would be following a full workshop model. This was perfect in kindergarten. It allowed me to slowly introduce the stations, while also starting groups and establishing my expectations for the class time. Students never had to wonder what they were doing, and instead, they were able to effectively run the Daily 5 model. My love for the Daily 5 eventually waned, but the basis of using the first 20 days of school to develop the routines and procedures never did.

When I transitioned from kindergarten to fourth grade, I wanted to continue the 20-day model from kindergarten. However, I quickly found it to be too much in upper elementary. While the 20 days were incredibly beneficial for five- and six-year-olds, upper elementary students had already had four years of experience, at least, with the reading workshop model. This was especially true if students were in the same district or county all their school life, and all teachers were expected to follow the workshop model. Fourth, fifth, and sixth graders knew what to expect from the workshop model; they learned how to run a little faster than my kindergarteners. So, what took my kindergarteners 20 days was only taking my older students about 10 days to master.

I'm not saying that you need to take exactly 10 days to establish your literacy block. Instead, listen to the needs of your students and have a plan for going a little faster or slowing things down as needed. To help get your ideas flowing and give you a starting point to jump off from, let's take a close look at what establishing your literacy block could look like with a variety of options that range from 5 to 20 days. Keep in mind the different elements that were discussed in Chapter 1 for crafting your block. Here are some other lesson ideas to consider:

- Choosing a Just-Right Book
- Building Reading Stamina
- Finding a Reading Spot
- Recording the Books You Read
- Keeping Your Eyes on Your Book the Whole Time

As you look over the images of example lessons (see Figure 2.3), all of which are given to you by visiting www.buildingtheliteracyblockresources.com, there are a few components that need to be pointed out to better help you understand the method behind the madness. The first component is the importance of accessing materials and establishing the norm of the classroom. Just because students know how to read does not mean they are avid

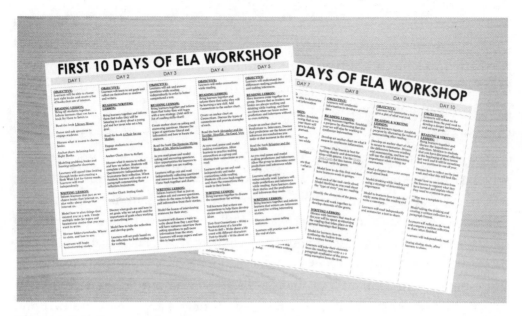

Figure 2.3 Lesson plans.

readers. This is something that needs to be addressed, discussed, and modeled for students at every age. That is why there are a few days, depending on the lesson plan you are looking at, that consist of selecting just-right books, finding a spot to read, and tracking the books read. All these lessons combine to help ensure that students know the expectations and feel successful no matter the type of reader.

Quick Tip: If you are looking for ways to increase your classroom community and library awareness, have your students organize your library with you (see Figure 2.4)! As a kindergarten teacher, I took this challenge on and we spent about two days working on creating categories that made sense for them. It was an incredibly rewarding experience. If having students reorganize your entire library is too chaotic, then have them help identify categories that can be incorporated sporadically throughout your library. For example, I organize my library based on genres. At the beginning of the year, I have students discuss some categories they enjoy. We locate the books and place them into a bin, and I have a student create the label for that category. We change these throughout the year to keep students interested and learning about new book options.

The second component is based around having students get to know themselves as readers and writers. While most students will do this each year and it may seem repetitive, there is something to be said about consistent reflection. Even as a teacher, reflection allows for us to understand our needs better and celebrate the advancements that we have made. We want to incorporate this as much as possible in our lessons with students. Spend some time giving out surveys, having discussions about where they like to sit, what they like to read, and strategies to help keep them focused and

Figure 2.4 Student categories for library.

build stamina. In writing, this is a time to teach learners how to brainstorm story ideas and give them opportunities to be creative. The more you have conversations around the differences there are between readers and writers, the more confident your students will become.

The third component is to incorporate lessons on reading and writing skills that will be discussed during the school year. Don't confuse this time for jumping into content lessons, instead look at this as an opportunity to review language that students have previously learned. Discuss what it means to track your thinking, to make connections, to ask questions, to visualize, and to make inferences. Develop a system for having students track and discuss these thoughts as they read. I prefer the simplicity of a sticky note because it's quick and doesn't require students to write a lot of information. These quick lessons are nice to define purpose to their independent reading time, and it gives you a base for future lessons. During your closing circle, have students share some of their thoughts from their independent reading that day. This is a great time to get students talking about their books even if you don't know what they are reading. You can always ask follow-up questions to get a better understanding of the story, and it makes your students feel a sense of pride of independence.

Choosing between the Right Number of Days

Knowing the right number of days for establishing your literacy block may seem a little overwhelming, but there are a few tips that can offer a little more guidance. Every situation can be different, and this means you need to fully consider your school, students, and your own preferences. There is nothing wrong with taking lessons you find online or that are provided by your school to help you establish your reading block. However, in order to gain a firm grasp of your block, you must truly understand the purpose of each component. Only then, will you have a better understanding of how to help your students grow.

Backward Planning

Before the beginning of the year, take some time to do a little backward planning. If you are new to the grade level or a new teacher in general, you might want to get a veteran teacher involved to help you with this process. Backward planning is exactly what the name suggests; it is the idea of planning from the end and working your way forward. Before you start planning out your units, take your school calendar and any events that you know may occur throughout the year and begin penciling them into your own calendar. When you know the conflicts that will take you away from your instruction you will be able to plan accordingly and ensure that you are meeting all the standards for the year. It may also be helpful to think about any additional celebrations, half days, assessments or school events that will interfere with your instruction. While you may not know the exact date on which you will hold the event, you can at least place a tentative marker on your calendar so that you can account for it during your planning.

> **Quick Tip:** Keep a list of these events in a Google Doc or using a note-taking app on your phone. As the year progresses, make additional notes so that next year your planning will be more precise. You can even add an estimated date on or month in which the event occurs.

Once you have your dates logged, think about when your final day of instruction will be. You might want to give yourself some wiggle room by adding in some buffer dates. If you are like me and work with units of study, think about adding two to five days at the end of each unit just in case something gets thrown off on your schedule. When you have your final date of instruction, with buffer dates included, then start thinking about how long your units of study will take you. Plan each unit by using a highlighter and marking the days off that will be used for instruction. As you move on to different units, you can change colors to help make this process even more visual. This process of backward planning will help you understand what is realistic for your class to begin their literacy block. When you get to the beginning of your calendar, you should have some days left that will make up your establishing workshop mini unit.

Getting the Timing Right

Have you ever tried to stand at the gas pump and stop at a rounded number like $50? I have, and it's near impossible; it never fails that I have that pesky $.01 at the end. Getting your own timing right in your classroom is just the same. You will constantly try and get it the first try, but you will always be off by a little. This is expected because so much of what can happen in our day is unexpected. There are a few things to consider when thinking about how much time is right for establishing your block.

- How long is your literacy block?
- Do you have alternate days when you teach reading and writing?
- Are you able to combine reading and writing instruction to save time and build a more integrated approach?
- Are you sharing the time with teachers who conduct some form of pull-out instruction?

If you have two hours in your block, you can ideally have two mini-lessons in one day compared to other teachers who can only have one. This might mean that you are able to hit those key elements for establishing your block much sooner than others. Find the perfect balance with how much time you need and what is realistic for your schedule. You might have to make a choice between which lessons are most essential and which ones you can easily weave into your block to build success.

The Must-Dos and Nice-to-Haves

As much as we try to be superheroes and do everything for ourselves and others, it isn't sustainable. It is unrealistic to think we can fit everything in our schedule. As you begin looking at what elements that need to be included when establishing your literacy block, you need to consider which elements you must teach versus what would be nice to teach. Creating a list of items for setting up your block will help to define your priorities. It will also ensure that you are targeting your instruction with what you need the most. It keeps you from straying and it will build a successful literacy block where students can learn and grow.

Grading Assignments

Depending on your school requirements, you may need to consider any grades that are taken during the first few weeks of school. Follow up with your school on what the requirements are during the first month of school. While it is still possible to collect grades, the first few days are more about routines and procedures than collecting content-based assignments. If you need to gather grades, it may greatly impact the amount of time you are able to take for establishing your block.

Considering Requirements

Finally, you will need to identify the non-negotiables that are dictated by your school or district. For example, your school may require a word study component, and in this case, you might have to incorporate additional lessons to ensure students understand the proper routine. This can be part of developing your must-dos and nice-to-haves, but it is always worth mentioning.

Chapter Wrap-Up

Your literacy block, no matter the allotted time, has the potential to be successful with proper planning. As you begin planning your time and the elements to include in your block, remember that your ideal block may not come to fruition. You might have to take additional time or even re-establish your block at various points in the school year. There is no one-size-fits-all process, and this means that you will have to take what you've read, and adapt it to fit your and your students' needs. After reading this chapter, prioritize the following steps for working toward the ultimate ELA workshop:

- Determine how many days you can dedicate to establishing your literacy block.

- Create your list of must-dos and nice-to-haves lessons for establishing your literacy block.

- Identify how you plan to scaffold the lessons to build confidence in your students.

- Begin backward planning to identify how much time you really need.

3 | Do the Work, Work, Work

What did teachers do before Pinterest or Instagram? My first year of teaching coincided with the launch of Instagram and Pinterest. While in school for my bachelors, I spent hours looking through blog posts of teachers who were sharing the exciting things they were doing in their classrooms. The internet and social media took collaboration worldwide and I loved the idea of taking a virtual peek inside of the classrooms of teachers I admired. It expanded my creative thinking, and it forced me to view new ways of instructing my class. I felt like if those teachers could do it, so could I.

Fast-forward to my first year teaching fourth grade, I was completely lost. I mentioned in a previous chapter how I would spend hours online looking for resources, guides, and examples that could help me structure my classroom. Pinterest and Instagram were my constant companions in those early times of teaching ELA. During one of my scrolls through Instagram, I was in search of something to help me track what my students were reading during their independent time, a common frustration for many upper elementary teachers.

At this stage in my teaching, I understood the importance of independent reading, but I struggled with managing students during this time. How do you know what they are reading? How do you know that they are reading the required 20 minutes each day? These were questions that I and likely every teacher has thought of at some point in their careers. My questions and search took me to someone online who was using a system called Status of the Class (I later realized this system came from Donalyn Miller's book *Reading in the Wild*). Each day the teacher would ask for the students to tell her what page and book they were on at the start of class. The teacher would record the answers in a simple calendar where each student had their own page. That's it! Only once, and it could give a wealth of information. The teacher could then track how many pages students were reading and whether they were finishing (or abandoning) books.

I utilized this seemingly simple idea, but it didn't work for long. The primary issue was my own fault. I didn't do anything with the information. Instead, the calendars sat inside of a binder, and I never looked at it other than a quick glance as I was recording the next day's information. What good is that? The second issue was that this system felt cold and detached from showing my students that I cared about them as readers. It was not feasible to meet with each student individually, so at the start of the class, I called their name. This felt like a roll call for reading. This made us fall into the trap of routine without purpose. Finally, the process of Status of the Class became too much work, and paper, to handle. It took up valuable time in class and was not benefiting students or me in any way. Knowing what my students were reading could have been approached in a different way, but it took me some time to find this out.

We, as teachers, must get into the regular practice of questioning why we do things. This isn't to be defiant toward our administrators or those who create our lesson or show annoyance to change, but rather to show that we care about how we spend our time in the classroom. Each minute is precious, and therefore, we have to figure out how to best utilize that time to benefit our students. After a couple of months, I started to question my reasons for implementing Status of the Class in the first place.

After what felt like an endless search, I realized that the approaches I was looking for didn't exist. I realized the community of readers and writers that

I wanted to build was nonexistent. That's when I found Miller's book *Reading in the Wild*. I wanted to create a classroom of readers that she wrote about. I hoped to build a classroom of students who loved to read, engaged in discussion, and shared their thoughts about stories in class. Only, I felt further from this reality than when I had initially started my search. What we see online, while it can be incredibly inspiring, needs to be taken with a grain of salt and questioned. In fact, this very book you are reading should be questioned!

I went back to the drawing board shortly after stopping Status of the Class, and I referenced what I consider to be the bible to student independence: *Leaders of Their Own Learning* by Ron Berger. This book embodied everything I thought learning should be, and I worked to bring this into my own classroom. I had first learned of this book while teaching kindergarten. My then assistant principal was passionate about the messaging, and it all stuck with me as I continued my career.

The biggest idea from Berger was that of placing students in the driver's seat of their own learning. Yes, I could teach them to read, identify the main idea, and write down a few sentences, but without the intrinsic passion for learning and using this to better themselves, what is the point? I wanted to make a bigger difference in my students. This meant that all those ideas, strategies, and resources needed to be questioned and determined if it still aligned with my vision. It's funny how, when you are in the thick of teaching, it can be so easy to lose track of your goals. The fact that something is cute or looks fun can easily pull you off of your path. This was true in my own case.

This experience led me to find better solutions. I began working on incorporating the elements that I had started back with my kindergarten class. I know what you are thinking: *kindergarten strategies in fourth grade; how is that possible?* Independence is something that translates across all ages, and in order to build independence, there must be some essential components: meeting with students, giving feedback, being consistent, making connections, and building trust. Remember, this isn't about doing all the things; it's about doing the right things that will help students grow and feel successful.

Building Blocks to Student Independence

Creating a classroom where students are driven by their success in learning and where they *want* to succeed is every teacher's dream. However, this is not a reality for many teachers. In our classrooms, we find students who are struggling with completing assignments, staying on task, and who simply do not care nor put forth their best effort. How do we overcome the barriers that our students put up to help them recognize that they can grow and succeed in their own learning?

From my experience, we have to show students that we care about where they are in their learning and break through the standard classroom design, in which the teacher is the sole provider of information and the student is responsible for consuming this knowledge. When we do this, our students will thrive in and outside of the classroom. Our job is to guide them to be the heroes of their own stories. If you are a *Star Wars* fan, you can imagine yourself as Yoda and each student as Luke Skywalker; sounds pretty cool, right? In order to build independence, we must allow them to make choices, and our role is to ensure they can make the *right* choices for their learning journey. Sounds great in theory, but you might be asking how this is possible.

Think about the first time your parents gave you more freedom. I'm sure our experience with this varies depending on your family, and that we each experienced freedom at different points in our lives. It may have been the freedom to choose what you got to wear. It may have been the freedom to go to a friend's house, or even to drive a car or ride a bike to school. I'd almost bet that freedom did not come without some direction from parents or guardians. This freedom also came with making some mistakes. We all made them, but it was the lessons that we were able to learn from those mistakes that allowed us to grow and make better choices in the future. If you would have walked out of your bedroom with sweatpants, a tutu, and a bike helmet, your parents didn't remove the right to choose your clothes, you simply learned and tried again. The choices you made in your wardrobe as a kid, the choices in music, friends, or even your actions were not dictated by anyone but yourself. You have full control, just as your students have full control over the choices they make in the classroom. Our jobs are to help students learn about the choices they can make in their learning and to help them try again when they make mistakes.

Now, I'd like to address centers before moving on to discuss how we can start building independence in our classrooms. Classroom centers have been a debate among teachers for many years. Some will swear by them, and others despise them. My feeling is that literacy centers prevent you from building independence. While I believe that there is such a thing called limited choice, centers prohibit students from making choices based on where they are in their own learning. Centers are dictated by the teacher, and during my years as a kindergarten teacher, I found that adding activities into each center did not allow for individual choice because my students all had different needs. I was not only limiting their learning, but I was also spending nights and weekends creating resources that I thought would help them grow. I was wrong. Instead, I decided to scrap the idea of centers altogether and gave my students choice. We developed data binders to help them pinpoint what they needed, and I supplied resources. Soon, I would have students making choices on learning new sight words from their personalized lists so that they could get a gold star. I had students working on their writing more, and others who were practicing reading from their personalized book bags. When I gave my kinders choice, they took it and flew.

If we are constantly dictating what students do and when they do it, we are creating learners who are dependent on their teacher. Literacy centers are the perfect example of creating an environment of learners who rely on the commands of their teachers. While organized, centers do not allow for choice that is substantial enough to model and create independence. The choice we give them in their learning is about their individual needs. If you love this idea of offering more choice, I have an entire chapter in Part 3 of this book that will guide you in creating this in your own classroom. You can reference Chapter 7 for creating goals.

We understand the importance of choice, but there are many other elements that will support your students in the process of leading their own learning. Remember that this is not an exhaustive list, but rather the pieces that I have found to be the most crucial when creating this environment. As you read each of the following elements, reflect on your routines and procedures, and find ways to embed this into your schedule. As I share each one, I offer ideas on how to implement and manage these so that you and your students can feel successful. Before you say, *my students can't do that*, I want you to know that it is possible from both a kindergarten and Title 1 school perspective. All you have to do is stay positive and have faith in your students.

Making Connections

Helping students see the connection between literacy and their own lives can seem daunting. After all, we don't have the ability to create word problems using student names or real-world problems in order to teach a concept, and writing short stories for each student just doesn't seem feasible. However, there are methods for connecting aspects of literacy instruction to what students might experience in their own lives. One of my favorite examples in upper elementary is creating this idea that I, the teacher, am the judge. As students go to answer questions or share about their independent readings at the end of class, they will have to give as much information as possible to help me understand the evidence they have located in their readings, the importance of the evidence, and the story that is taking place. Now, many students do not aspire to be a judge or lawyer, but when I make the connection to asking their parents if they can go somewhere or do something, they understand the format of building a compelling argument. That's right, I am teaching my students how to get everything they want.

This is only one way that I incorporate connection in my classroom, and if you are wondering whether I create an entire classroom setup to make it look like a courtroom, I haven't. I keep it very simple and ask kids to argue their point. I might also have some fun giveaways for students who knock my socks off. The following are some other ideas for how you can create connections for your students:

- **Connect skills to things outside of the classroom.** When we teach students to read in upper elementary, they are learning about the best strategies for developing skills as readers and writers. Examples of such skills include inferring, visualizing, questioning, summarizing, and so on. Prior to starting a lesson, hook your students by giving them a real-world experience where they can relate to the skill before they try and implement it in their reading. Keep these short (half or one whole class period), and more importantly, go back and reference this experience as you make the connection to their reading. Here are some examples to get you started:

  - Create a crime scene where students have to infer what happened (see Figure 3.1).

  - Have students share something they did over the weekend without elaborating on the events. The other members of the class will then ask questions to pull as much information to understand what happened.

  - Have students summarize their morning or weekends.

- **Connect reading to other subjects.** Choosing reading material is one of the easiest ways to relate what they do as readers and writers to their own lives and to other areas of their learning. It is also often overlooked because we get comfortable with the texts we use in our lessons. This is a reminder to be OK with getting uncomfortable and branch outside of the same old texts, and find texts that connect to other subject areas or to situations that are occurring in their own lives. It always amazes me when I pull out a social studies or science text and a student tells me that this is a reading class. When we connect the subject areas, they are more likely

Figure 3.1 Crime scene.

to connect the skills and strategies you are teaching to their other classes. Your colleagues will thank you.

- **Connect to other goals.** Teaching students how to set goals is one of my favorite topics. Goal setting is something that will constantly support them in anything they do. So even with fourth graders, I will sit down and discuss the difference between quantitative and qualitative data. I will have students share about goals they have outside of school, and we always take time to build community and celebrate when a student comes in excitedly and shares they mastered a new goal.

- **Connect to the importance of reading.** It is every teacher's dream to have a classroom filled with readers, but the process of getting students to willfully be readers can be challenging. At the beginning of the year, I like to show a YouTube video titled "Reading a Book a Week for 4 Years— This Happened." The person who recorded the video shares why he started reading a book a week, his journey to being able to read a book a week, and the results that stemmed from it. This video, while so simple, makes a huge impact with my students. We talk about goals, and how we too can achieve the results he had, and more importantly it is someone other than a teacher telling them that reading is good. I highly encourage you to check out the video at: bit.ly/ReadABookAWeek.

- **Connect 21st-century skills to their interests.** Teaching students to read and write is so much more than summarizing or determining the main idea of a text; it is also about teaching students the skills and strategies for being successful. This means that students must learn to be organized, manage their time well, ask for help when needed, problem-solve, and more. While most of our instruction focuses on reading and writing, we must also model how to be successful using these skills. Connect to these skills and how it benefits them as learners and in other areas of life. This is a great time for students to share experiences with topics they enjoy. For instance, they can share about how they use grit in a sport they play, or how they had to problem-solve when they were trying to make a fort in their backyards. Model what they are doing, discuss the relevance, and create a connection between school and life.

Making connections does not need to happen each week. However, you can introduce a skill in this way and be mindful to make connections to it as you are giving instruction. For instance, you can use language such as *remember when we . . ., even when we . . ., we . . . .* These simple references will help students see the importance and value of learning a new skill or strategy. You can also have students help create a list of ways they can utilize these skills outside of school. You'd be surprised by what they come up with.

Conferring with Students

Our growth as individuals come from different avenues of our lives. One of those avenues are the connections and guidance that we have with those around us. This can come from a parent who offers advice and support, a teacher who spends extra time to reteach challenging concepts, or an idol who shares their experiences so that others can learn from his/her mistakes.

These moments in our life are what propels ideas to lead to action. Our students also want and need this in order to continue growing. Incorporating student-teacher conferences in your classroom is a great way to create this sense of belonging. You might think that you don't have enough time or don't know where to start. Luckily, there is an entire chapter dedicated to helping you master the art of conferring with students. Chapter 6 offers strategies, tips, and tools for incorporating conferences at any level or timeframe. To get some of your brain juices flowing, the following are some simple tips for making conferences successful, and if you're thinking to yourself, *she repeats a lot of the same stuff in this book*, you're right. I do. I repeat things because it's important.

- **Start Small.** I have a "gung-ho" mentality and I will often throw myself into the thick of any new project and feel overwhelmed. Don't do this. If you are new to conferring, start by telling yourself that you will meet once with every student in one month and gradually shorten the timeframe. You'll start feeling successful and find your own rhythm to meeting with students.

- **Make a Plan.** Knowing what you are going to be discussing during your conferences is important. It defines purpose and allows you to stay on track timewise. As mentioned before, Chapter 6 provides you with the exact game-plan for a variety of conference types.

- **Create a Day.** Meeting with all your students during a specific time period can be hard especially if your schedule has been thrown off or if you've had to spend a little more time than normal learning a specific skill. One little trick that I like to have up my sleeve is to have a reflection day. On this day, students are working on answering an open-ended question discussing what they learned and how they can use the strategy in their own learning. This is also a time for students to complete any missing assignments or revise and resubmit if asked to do so. While students are working, use this time to meet with students independently for conferences. You'll be able to meet with more students than average days and your students will appreciate the additional time to complete assignments.

Giving Feedback

Grading papers is one of the largest, most daunting tasks for any teacher. Sometimes, it seems like enough to mark the things that are wrong and slap a grade on it at the end of the day, but what message are we sending students? On the other hand, one topic that has been the subject of debate among teachers is to simply throw away ungraded papers because you don't have the time or energy to give them a grade. While I can understand the premise behind throwing away a pile of papers that will take days to catch up on, I struggle with the message that it sends to students. This act of throwing away work tells students that the time and effort they put into their assignments is not important. Yes, it decreases teacher stress, but it is at the cost of students' motivation to do more. Instead, can you take a different approach to decrease the amount of grading you have as a teacher by asking the question: *Can we limit the amount of work students are doing to meaningful and relevant tasks?*

Giving feedback is one of the most time-consuming aspects of teaching, but it is also the most rewarding when it comes to creating student independence. This idea goes back to showing students that we care about them as individuals and as learners. We show that we value their time and want to support them to do their best each time. The positive effects of student feedback are clear, but it is often something we forget or skip purely because of how time-consuming it can be. There are not enough hours in the day. Therefore, you need to determine where your time is best served based on the goals you have for you and your students.

However, there are many ways in which you can successfully provide feedback. Being intentional with your daily assignments is a great start. Determine how many assignments you are giving during a typical class period. Categorize these assignments; for example: exit tickets, discussion boards, reading response, word study sort, and so on. This will give you a general idea of the amount of work you are creating for your students and for yourself. Now think if there are other methods that can be effective and much more meaningful without the added workload of grading. For example, whiteboards allow me to quickly assess my students' thinking and give immediate feedback as I walk around and check their answers. Done. In less than five minutes students know where they stand with that activity. The lesson? Be mindful of what you give your students. If you don't have time to grade or give feedback, find another way that you can assess their understanding. Here are some other ideas for giving efficient feedback:

- **Create meaningful rubrics.** Rubrics are time-consuming, but if you can tag team them with your grade-level partners, then they are well worth the effort (see Figure 3.2). However, it may be beneficial to consider creating rubrics for assessing certain skills or strategies versus assignment. The idea is that you can use these rubrics for multiple assignments versus just one. For example, if I need to assess my students' abilities to use evidence, I will create a rubric on just that component and either use it for a targeted assignment or add it on to a larger project. This will give you flexibility with your rubric and it will also create purpose.

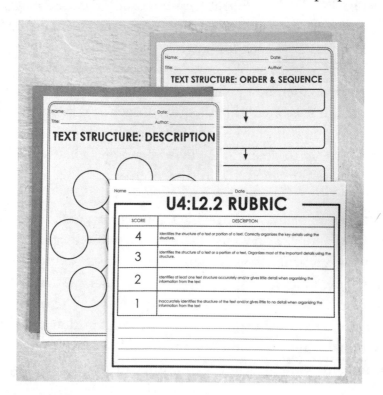

Figure 3.2 Rubrics.

- **Use voice memos within your LMS.** Sometimes it is easier if you leave a voice memo. Many schools are beginning to see the value of using a learner management system (LMS) such as Google Classroom, Schoology, or Canvas. Many have features that allow the teacher to record audio and allow students to listen. If you need to explain what they did and how to improve, leave a voice memo on their assignment. The student can then listen and ask additional questions if needed.

- **Meet with students during conferences.** Once you become a pro at meeting with students for conferences, use one of the days to discuss their work and give feedback in person. This creates a place where you can model strategies and allow students to ask questions.

- **Create a screen recording.** This is by far one of my favorite features. If you are an iPad/tablet user or can screen record on your laptop, give feedback on their assignment with a screencast. Here, you can do something like in-person conferences and model a particular strategy or point out areas that need revision. Share the video through email or LMS.

Be Consistent

You cannot expect your students to be independent if you do not model that yourself. You can't have expectations of the classroom, but rather of students or yourself. If you want students to be organized, you need to show them this by being organized yourself. If you want students to do their best work, then you must give them feedback. You have to hold yourself accountable in order to hold your students accountable for their own work. Consistency is the path to success. Here are some tips for creating consistency:

- Set goals for yourself to grow in your craft. Start small with one to two goals and then build from there.

- Set reminders on your phone when starting new routines. You'll need them to develop effective habits.

- Maintain a tracker next to your desk. This can be as simple as a calendar. Cross off days as you implement the new strategies in your teaching.

- Find an accountability buddy. This can be a partner teacher who has the same goal as you do!
- More than anything, be patient. You cannot expect for everything to go smoothly right from the beginning.

You will get busy and stray away from your goals, but it is your job to recognize that and continue to push through. It took me four years to deeply understand how to use learning targets in my classroom. It was something that I had to constantly work on, and eventually, it became second nature.

Build Trust

Finally, for your students to be independent, you must trust them. Will they make mistakes? Absolutely. However, we cannot judge them for their mistakes, instead we have to find ways to guide and support them so that they can be successful. If we dictate every move they make in our classrooms, students will know that we lack trust in their decisions. It can be so easy to make all their choices for them, but when students make mistakes they are able to learn and grow from those experiences. It is through their failures that we learn how to help them. It is through their failures that we move forward.

One of my all-time favorite picture books is called *Jonanthan James and the Whatif Monster* by Michelle Nelson-Schmidt. It's a simple read but the message resonates with me. It is a story about a young boy who worries about everything. As a fellow worrywart, I will often think about the whatif monster when I start anything new. So, to help overcome the whatif monster, I have compiled a few questions you may have as it pertains to building and trusting student independence.

- **What if a kid doesn't turn in their work?** Create a check-in. Meet with the learner during an individual conference and discuss your concern about them missing assignments and why they might be struggling. Set up a game plan and define times and days that you will check in to help them succeed. As the student gets better at submitting work, you can decrease your check-ins with them.

- **What if they are not reading independently?** Determine what you are trying to have the learner read and identify the problem. Is the student a struggling reader? Is the book too advanced? Is there a lack of interest in the topic? Instead of making the student complete written work to establish accountability, define the problem, create a solution, and maintain check-ins. You can have the learner start with picture books, audio books, or find a book that you think might be of interest. Check in with the student during conferences to discuss how the book is going and reevaluate whether they need a different book.

- **What if they are struggling with incomplete or sloppy work?** Again, define the problem. Is the workload too overwhelming? Does the learner have a disability that makes the work challenging? Start by limiting the number of sentences they have to write or questions they have to answer. Maybe instead of four vocabulary words, the learner has one or two they need to complete. If they have sloppy work, then offer other modes for demonstrating their learning. Perhaps they can type it or complete an audio recording explaining their answer. Start there and slowly work up to completing the entire assignments and in various formats.

- **What if they don't want to do the work?** There is a reason behind every behavior. Get the student started by pulling a small group that can use additional support at the end of the lesson. Provide audio recordings of the readings or discuss the questions prior to the learner completing the assignment independently. The cause for this is the students' own feeling of failure. Help them succeed by giving them the right tools.

- **What if they are disrupting others?** Disruption is a result from many of the behaviors that we have previously talked about in the preceding bullets. Identify where they struggle in their learning and find ways to help them succeed. Move their seats near you. Have check-ins that will create a safe space for them to share questions. Have this learner be part of the small group you pull to give additional assistance.

Chapter Wrap-Up

Building independence takes time, but if we all choose to help students see the value of learning and give them the tools to be successful, we can develop lifelong learners. While you may not be able to have every child in your classroom become totally independent, the goal is to show some improvement based on where they started. If you can define how they have changed from the beginning of the year to the end, you have made a difference. After reading this chapter, consider the following steps on getting started with successfully building independent learners:

- Look through your curriculum and identify the lessons in which you can incorporate connections.

- Work with your grade-level team to create meaningful rubrics based on reading and writing skills, not assignments.

- Look at a calendar for the first full month of school. Place student names on each school day, and plan to meet with them for an individual conference.

- Go back to your establishing workshop plans and incorporate 21st-century skills that are necessary for students throughout the year. This can be organizing, time management, problem solving, and more.

PART

II | The Strategies

Going through college and learning about how to be a teacher is one of the most exciting moments in our careers. We dream of the day that we can decorate our own classrooms, create our own lessons, and excite and engage our students in learning. No matter where you are in your career, you will always remember these years. Going into that first year of teaching, you work to create a space that welcomes students on the first day of school.

Once in the thick of teaching, you quickly realize that this is nothing like you envisioned. You have little to no time for you, your family, or friends. You are overwhelmed with paperwork, prepping materials, and lesson planning. You struggle with how to format your lessons and are unfamiliar with the content. Dealing with behaviors (of both students and parents) can be intimidating, and you wish you'd done more to feel prepared. Teaching can be defeating when you don't have the proper strategies to help guide you, and despite what most universities try to do, many first-year teachers feel ill-prepared to run a classroom.

However, the same can be said about veteran teachers. Many educators have felt at some point in their careers trapped in the workloads of papers, forms, and behaviors. Many others feel like they've spent years developing their craft and style for teaching. Only, it can be easy to lose sight and feel as though you have fallen into a repetitive cycle. It can cause you to feel closed inside of a box, with no fresh or new perspectives. You get stuck into the mundane tasks that no longer excite you or bring you joy. You lose your passion and begin to question whether you were meant to be a teacher at all, and let's face it, it can be easy to hand out a worksheet and slap a grade on it at the end of the day. Is this really what you envisioned when you wanted to be a teacher?

I've been that first-year teacher who felt overwhelmed, and I've also felt stuck without vision for what I wanted my literacy block to look and sound like. Knowing strategies that will guide your teaching is invaluable. These strategies will help to guide the instruction you give to your students; it will keep you sane in the busy seasons, and it will keep your students engaged and excited about learning. Your strategies are your go-to constant, but as you work with these strategies you will find methods for placing your own personal twist on them. There will be strategies you like to use more than others and some that may not work for your teaching style, but the fact of the matter is that you are willing to try them and make them your own.

As you work through these next few chapters try and keep an open mind. It can be easy to say that *this doesn't work for my kids*, or *I don't have any time for that*. I guarantee you that this is possible for any teacher, and I will offer some alternatives as we move through the strategies. My time with Title 1 students, English language learners, learning support, gifted students, and diverse communities has shown me the possibilities that good and authentic teaching strategies have on learning, and the chapters that follow are about the realities of teaching and how to make them engaging and purposeful for your students but also manageable from the teacher's perspective.

I often tell other teachers that I am a lazy teacher; not in literal terms, but to say that I like to work smarter not harder. I use the same resources, strategies, and activities repeatedly because I know they work. This might seem mundane, but the magic is where you sprinkle in the small changes that give enough variation to how you implement your lessons and engage your students. Many of the strategies are simple enough that they can be implemented at various points during the school year. Use this to your advantage because the more you reuse strategies, the easier it will be for your students to focus on the learning versus how to place an activity or use a particular organizer. Making too many changes will confuse your students and negatively affect their learning.

Another component of my lazy teacher persona is about getting students involved in their learning. The more work they are doing, the lazier I can be (again, I mean this figuratively, not literally). Chapter 3 discusses how to build independent learners; much of the work in these next three chapters is a continuation of this concept. When you have your students doing more, they are taking on the role of being independent thinkers and learners. This will place less stress on you as a teacher because your role changes from providing the learning to facilitating the learning.

While you read through the next few chapters, spend time reflecting on your practices now. How can you begin to incorporate some of these elements? This may mean revisiting how you structure your lessons or the types of assignments you are giving students to assess their learning. The hope is that if you are the new teacher who needs additional support to guide you through your first year, this section is for you. In addition, if you are a veteran teacher who feels stuck in the same old lessons that don't engage and excite, then this section is for you. No matter where you are in your career, there are always going to be opportunities for growth. So, let's get started on this journey together and make a bigger impact in literacy instruction.

4 | Follow the Yellow Brick Road

The school that I joined for six years of my teaching career was amazing, but it lacked resources to help guide teachers in developing authentic and rigorous instruction. Honestly, it expected its teachers to do this, and while it may have seemed frustrating to most, it was one of the most freeing and worthwhile experiences. It made me think, caused me to go outside of the box, and allowed me to explore various methods for teaching and failing forward if needed. I knew that despite the stress, I would leave a better teacher because of my time at this school.

Now, I didn't always feel this way. In fact, there was a time where everything felt like it was in shambles. I was having some health issues, my partner was diagnosed with cancer, and I was an emotional mess about 99.9% of the time. I could barely think about my lessons and what the next day was going to look like. I felt as though myself and my other team partner were always treading water. So, when it came to creating lessons and engaging students in their learning, many things started to fall by the wayside.

I was good at teaching reading—that had always been my strongest area of instruction—but science and social studies was the expertise of our partner who had fallen ill. She was a creative mastermind. When she was no longer there, we felt as though we had no other option but to scroll the internet for resources, activities, and lessons to guide our instruction. Our instruction during those final three months of school felt like a new driver in a different country. We could never see the exit to move on and everything started to blur together.

Online marketplace, Teacher Pay Teachers, and websites like Pinterest have made locating resources and finding ideas for teaching concepts in our class-room easy. So easy, in fact, that it has created this crutch that many teachers will use when they are unsure of what, when, or how to teach. I am not here to bash these sites; I love them! I use them every year, and I have found sell-ers who have opened new doors in my own teaching practices. What I want to drive home is that, as teachers, we need to be intentional with our searches. We need to know the goal of the lesson and the steps to ensure your students understand the concept. We need to know our *why*. When we can define the why behind the lesson, then we define where we are going and what we need as teachers. When we know our *why*, our *what* becomes much easier to understand.

Let's make this idea of knowing your why a little more relatable, in this case, let's think about driving to your school. Your why is going to work and the path is the route you take each day. There are probably plenty of ways you can drive there, but whether each of those routes is the most logical and efficient is left to argument. You have one path that you take each morning and afternoon. It is the same driving path because you have found that it gets you home the quickest. Each of the other routes are distractions; they take you longer to get to your destination, and while they may have a beau-tiful scenic view, you also have a greater chance of getting lost because you don't know those paths well enough.

Teaching literacy is like having a path every day that you follow. If you veer off in another direction, you take longer with getting to the point of the lesson or distract from the purpose altogether. However, having that clear path will stand as your yellow brick road. It will guide you through each lesson in the quickest, most efficient way possible. Your path in literacy will be the systematic routine that is used to structure each lesson. While this may seem mundane, your scenery will change from the corn fields to the apple orchards to the field of flowers. Your path is important, and in literacy, we call it the mini-lesson.

The Mini-Lesson Structure

Every literacy teacher has had some experience with the mini-lesson. Whether you are new to it or you've been using it for years, the mini-lesson is the structure of every whole-group lesson from kindergarten to the upper grades. However, many teachers continue to struggle with the timing, engagement, and overall structure for how to craft an effective mini-lesson. For over a decade, I worked to find the perfect structure of a mini-lesson, and most recently, how these mini-lessons look in an upper elementary classroom.

This systematic routine will help define how you teach each lesson and will allow your students to stop thinking about what they need to be doing and start focusing more on the learning that is taking place. While it may seem mundane to you, your students will benefit greatly from the structure. As you continue through the book, you will find ways to make the mini-lesson more engaging and collaborative so that your students stay interested in each lesson.

First, let's take a deep dive into the mini-lesson. One of the easiest methods for crafting an effective mini-lesson is to utilize the best practices for how students learn and retain new information. The gradual release of responsibility is a proven method for demonstrating, prompting, and allowing students to practice a specific skill or strategy for that lesson. Now, I am from the South (Texan born and raised, and lived in Alabama for 10 years), and during my years in the South, an additional component was added: Y'all Do. I'll explain the importance of this additional step later.

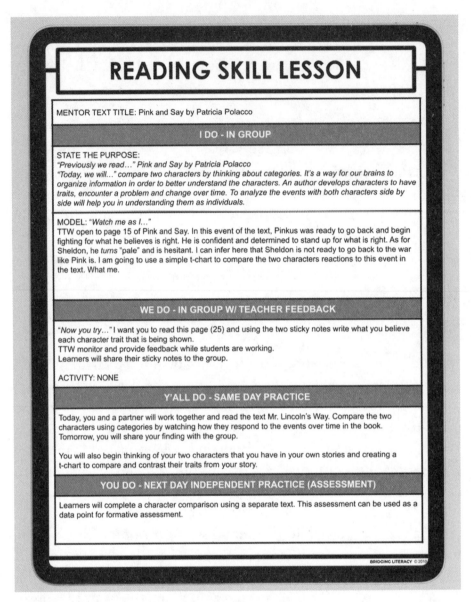

Figure 4.1 Example Minilesson.

You may be wondering how you fit all components of the gradual release model into what is meant to be a 15- to 20-minute mini-lesson. Well, as we dig deeper into better understanding each of the components, I share how this will look inside of a mini-lesson that I have taught several times in my own classroom (see Figure 4.1). At the end of this, I offer some essential tips for ensuring your mini-lesson runs smoothly.

I Do

Within your mini-lesson the first five minutes should be dedicated to the I Do portion of the gradual release model. This section is the explicit model of a specific skill or strategy, and it is where you think aloud as you share your process or strategy for accomplishing the learning target. The wording during this part of the mini-lesson should be concise. For example, instead of saying, *"As we read through this page of the book, you will want to look for times when the character is showing some form of feeling toward what is happening in the book,"* say *"On page 8, the characters feel _____ because I can infer it in this sentence."* Both explanations are about the characters feelings, but the latter gets to the point much quicker than the former. This is important because you don't want your students to get lost in translation. Be intentional with your words and give them a step-by-step model of the strategy.

During this portion of the model, there are a few key elements that you will want to include. The first is sharing the objective or learning target of the day. If you use an essential question for units of study or specific books, you will also want to reference the essential question in the beginning as well. For example, looking at the preceding lesson, you will notice that the teacher states *"yesterday we ___, and today we ___."* The purpose is clearly defined by telling students the objective of understanding character traits by looking closely at categories of what the character thinks, says, does, and feels. Setting the purpose should take no more than a minute of your I Do portion of the mini-lesson.

The next element consists of students observing as you model a specific strategy. Be concise with what you want to show your students, and you will want to, preferably, have read this text at a separate time or different day. Prior to the lesson, prepare a few items to ensure that this time doesn't drag on for too long. Here are some things to consider when planning this portion of the mini-lesson:

- Know the objective and the strategy that students will need to know.
- Have page numbers marked with a sticky note for easy reference.

- Have graphic organizers printed as posters or use a projector to model how to complete.

- Have certain parts of your organizer filled in but covered with a sticky note, and reveal the writing as you model. This cuts down on students watching you write.

- If using sticky notes, have those completed prior to the lesson.

We Do

The second portion of your mini-lesson consists of the *We Do* in the gradual release model. In this part, the role of the teacher diminishes, and students begin to give more input into how the strategy is implemented when reading or writing. The teacher, however, is still largely in control of the lesson, and as students begin to share, the teacher will offer support as needed. This portion of the mini-lesson should last anywhere from five to seven minutes. Think of this time as the moments when students begin turning and talking, answering questions, and getting a little more involved in the process.

Looking back at the example, focus on the fact that much of the talking and guiding is still coming from the teacher. The areas in which students are engaging in the lesson are limited but also purposeful. These areas that the teacher wants to ensure students can identify or analyze. For example, the teacher may want input on which piece of evidence best fits the strategy, or the teacher may want to know how to complete the topic sentence of a summary. When looking over your lesson, review the objective and identify the areas of the strategy that will be the most challenging. Have your students guide you through completing this process as you can offer support and give feedback.

Ideas for incorporating a We Do portion of the mini-lesson:

- Have learners help complete the sentence by identifying key words.

- Invite students to write their thoughts on the anchor chart or graphic organizer.

- Ask questions such as: "What do we do next?" or "When you read this what do you think of?"

- Allow students to write their thoughts on sticky notes and place them on the board.

- Have students use a whiteboard to display words, evidence, choices, and more for you to review.

Y'all Do

At this point in the lesson, you have had two opportunities to model how to use the strategy. The first was a model of your thinking through the process, and the second offered students the ability to participate in your thinking process. The Y'all Do section is about giving students the opportunity to collaborate with peers, and it can be done in three formats. The first is that this can happen during your mini-lesson and last from five to seven minutes. After modeling, you will inform students that they are going to have an opportunity to try the strategy or skill. The key to this is that students will be working in pairs during the activity. Students will be given a page of the reading, cards, organizers, sticky notes, or other materials to allow them to turn and have a conversation regarding the content. The teacher's role is about listening, questioning, and giving feedback as students work together. Feedback is a critical part of this process as it helps to inform students on whether they are understanding the concept. It is also a time for the teacher to determine which learners need to be pulled for additional instruction. This format is one that I would encourage teachers to do in their meeting area. If you can bring students to a carpet section, then students would simply turn and use their elbow partner, or if they are seated in pods at their desks, students could then use their pods for discussion. Limit the amount of movement because it will only cut into your time for small groups and conferences.

The second format to consider is to have students complete an activity as an extension of the lesson around the room with a partner or a small group. This can be beneficial especially if the topic that you are teaching is more complex and the We Do portion exceeds its timeframe. This will require movement and grouping based on whatever system you have (I share some ideas in Chapter 5). The teacher's role never changes. You are expected to be moving around the room making observations and providing feedback as needed. This is not a time to pull small groups and begin a separate portion of your lesson. Students need to have the feedback component to clarify misconceptions and ensure they are not practicing the strategy incorrectly.

A final format is in the form of an independent practice. This is when the teacher asks for learners to independently practice the strategy. The Y'all Do portion should be collaborative. It should allow for learners to have a conversation to listen to other ideas before moving on independently. If you have your students complete this section independently, make sure that they feel confident enough to try the strategy alone. This can be a very defeating time for some students because they are unsure where to start.

Ideas for incorporating a Y'all Do portion of the mini-lesson:

- Offer students a copy of a page from the book. Encourage students to highlight and write in the margins.
- Provide learners with a sort that contains information from the text. Remember to read or provide learners with a copy of the text.
- Have learners complete sentences by writing on a whiteboard or organizer.
- Provide learners with a graphic organizer to complete.
- Give learners multiple examples of a summary and ask students to determine which is the best and why.

You Do

The last portion of the lesson is an extension. The You Do section is about giving students the opportunity to complete the strategy independently after the mini-lesson is complete. At the end of the lesson, provide learners with a quick explanation of what they will be doing during their work time.

At this point, students have had three experiences with the strategy, and it is still relatively fresh in their minds. Provide learners with a new text or a portion of the mentor text that was not covered during the mini-lesson and allow students to implement the strategy. While I am fully aware that this activity is solo, I will, at times, allow students to continue working with one another, especially if the concept is challenging. Prior to giving this work to your students, decide on how and what you will be assessing. Make sure this is work that is purposeful and relevant to their growth as readers and writers, and have either a rubric or scoring criteria to support students with the process. If there is nothing to grade and you simply want an exit ticket, then articulate this information and collect and provide feedback so that students can make corrections for the next assignment. Since literacy work spirals, many of the strategies and skills are necessary to effectively do well in another task.

Many of the activity ideas are like the Y'all Do portion of the mini-lesson; however, there are some helpful tips for accommodating students at various points in their learning, and to help minimize your workload in the future.

- For learners with reading disabilities, provide a text on their level or record the reading prior to the day and have a QR code or link for them to listen.
- Have a rubric and answer key prepared in advance for quick and easy grading.
- Have sentence stems available for students who need additional support.
- If completing a detailed organizer, identify the question or elements students will need to consider when filling it in; this is especially helpful if students are completing a comparison chart. (An example of this is available at: bit.ly/THINKMARKS)

The lessons that you build for your students are all about gradually releasing the skills and strategies so that they feel confident and successful in their learning. This method of using the gradual release within your mini-lesson may not be new, but it isn't discussed enough. Take time to reflect on your lessons right now and decide how you can make changes based on the information I have given you in this chapter so far. Remember, you will not always be able to craft the perfect lesson. You will have times when you go over them (I still do this), and you will have to make adjustments, and that is OK. Find a rhythm that works best for you and your students.

To help give a little more context to when this lesson happens in my own classroom, I'll walk you through a series of events. When my students walk into the classroom, they are greeted with a message on the board that gives them a task to work on each day (you can reference Chapter 1 for ideas on your warm-up). After we have a chance to discuss, I hold a morning meeting. We review expectations, and I either give a book talk or have learners share their book talks to the class. Once finished, we have our mini-lesson. I prefer to have students come to a meeting area because I can ensure that they are all focused on me and the lesson. After that 15- to 20-minute mini-lesson, learners will get to work. Some will begin their independent component of that day's lesson, and others will be pulled to my small group table for additional support or conferences. This time-frame lasts for around 40 minutes. At the end of class, we will review the lesson objective, have students share their thoughts, and celebrate any wins from the day.

Tips for Crafting Your Mini-Lesson

As you continue to develop in your craft of constructing and implementing mini-lessons (see Figure 4.2) there are a few tips and reminders that may be helpful. The first is to utilize learning targets to define the intentions of the lesson and keep you and your students focused. Learning targets are student friendly "I can" statements that articulate the learning that needs to occur. These are not based on the product, but rather what learning students are expected demonstrate by the end of class. For example, *I can complete a graphic organizer on characters* is not an effective learning target because it states what students are physically doing. Instead, the learning target should

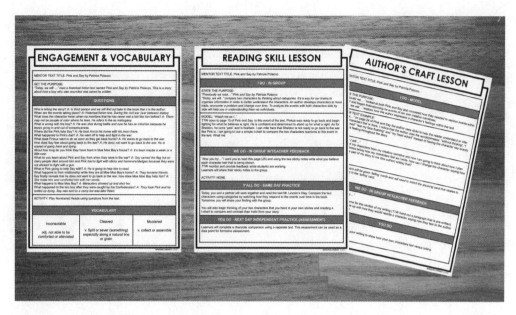

Figure 4.2 Different mini-lessons.

read: *I can compare and contrast two characters from a fictional text.* In this learning target, students have a clear understanding of the learning that is going to take place. You can ask the question: *What are we doing?* Learners should tell you that they are comparing in today's lesson. When you follow up with what they are comparing, learners should articulate characters in front of the same story. The emphasis is removed from the completion of a task and focused on what students are learning.

Learning targets also benefit you because it will keep you focused. I, like most other teachers, love a good teachable moment, but those moments can often derail you from the purpose of the lesson. Learning targets can help keep you focused during the lesson. If conversations begin to wander, have students look back at the learning target and evaluate whether it is beneficial to the objective of the day. I recommend having a location in your classroom where you can easily and quickly refer to your learning target during your lesson. This is not something to hide, but rather share with students so that they too can feel empowered in their learning. If you are required to have an essential question, have the question posted at the top and add

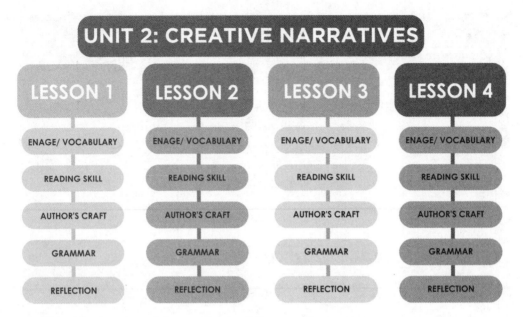

Figure 4.3 Bridging Literacy breakdown of one unit.

learning targets that will help support the essential question during the mini-lesson. You can discuss and make connections between the two as you teach your lesson.

My second tip for crafting mini-lessons is to break down the various types of lessons that you will need to teach at various points (see Figure 4.3). In kindergarten, I had a two-hour block for reading (my writing time was separate), and during this time, I started with a mini-lesson on phonemic awareness and letter recognition, then pulled a small group, then came back for a second mini-lesson on our sight words, then pulled a group, then followed that with a third mini-lesson on our comprehension skill, and finally pulled my remaining groups. It was a constant back and forth, but I had time to incorporate many types of lessons. When I moved to upper elementary, my time was cut in half and shared with intervention teachers. I realized that I could not have various lessons throughout the class time, and even more so, realized that I could not incorporate all the elements in one day. This is when I became strategic with my planning and crafted a method that I call the Bridging Literacy Method.

In the Bridging Literacy Method, I crafted six units of study that each revolve around a writing focus. Within each unit, reading skills are introduced that support the writing genre that students are studying. For instance, in the personal narrative unit, the reading skills focus on analyzing settings, asking questions, and supporting thinking using details from the text. These skills perfectly match the writing because students will use the learning to apply it to their own writing. In order to effectively plan out these lessons, each of the four reading skills were broken into five parts. For instance, each week we started with a lesson on asking questions, comprehension, and vocabulary. The second day consisted of learning the new reading skill and analyzing the mentor text from the day prior. On the third day, students apply their knowledge of the reading skill to a component in their writing; this might be during the brainstorming, writing, or revision section. On the fourth day, learners review grammar and word study, and they end the week with reflection and conferences.

Determine how to break down mini-lessons so that you can maintain focus. Do you have time to teach two lessons during your class period or will you need to use alternative methods to ensure you are covering all your standards? This could be through a method like Bridging Literacy or it could be with an A/B schedule. On A days, you might teach all your reading standards, and on B days, you might teach your writing lessons. You can also group and have four A days in a row and then follow it with four B days; whatever you choose, make sure it aligns with your schools' pacing guides and your teaching style.

If your school has a set curriculum that you are obligated to follow, there are ways in which you can take a little bit of the curriculum and a little of you to create realistic mini-lessons. For my curriculum teachers, my tip is to review the lessons and progression in advance. This is a great summer activity as it will limit your stress during the school year. Find ways to use the progression and lesson ideas as a guide rather than using it to fidelity. When I taught kindergarten, my school had Harcourt and the basal readers. I chose to not follow Harcourt to fidelity because so much of the lessons for comprehension felt random; for example, one day we would teach inferring, the next day would be on characters. For students who were English language learners, this concept of jumping comprehension strategies was far too difficult for them to understand. This is where I took concepts and lessons and used them to craft my own lessons. For some lessons I used the text they recommended, which came with the curriculum, and for others, I found a more suitable text that connected to our science and social studies time. Just remember that no curriculum out there, no matter how good it might seem, will ever meet the needs of all of your students.

Finally, as you are creating your mini-lessons, be mindful of the types of texts you are using (see Figure 4.4). This could be the genres that lend themselves to certain reading and writing lessons, but it could also be whether you choose to model the strategy with a poem, short story, chapter from a novel, or a picture book. When we are conscious of the types of

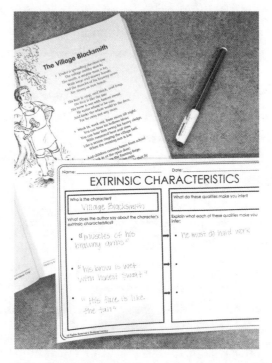

Figure 4.4 "The Village Blacksmith" poem excerpt with organizer.

texts that we are using to model strategies, it will help students see and learn the shifts necessary to think through the variations. You might model using a picture book but offer students a short story to work on for their independent practice; and poetry is not only useful for the month of April. It's important to show that all these forms of writing lend themselves to the skills we are learning in reading and writing. The more you make this evident in your lessons, the easier it will be for your students to apply their skills across a variety of texts.

Chapter Wrap-Up

Structuring your lessons is an integral component to ensuring that students feel successful and empowered in their own learning. There is no *one-size-fits-all* formula for crafting effective lessons, but there is science that shows the best forms for students to learn. The hope is that you can identify those elements in the gradual release model for crafting your mini-lesson. More than anything, take elements that work for you, your school, and your students, and incorporate them little by little. When you feel as though you have mastered one, add another element. This will not only create success for your students, but also for you as you begin planning more lessons. After reading this chapter, consider the following questions to guide you in implementing the new learning:

- Where will you hold your mini-lessons? Will it be a group meeting area or will students remain at their seats?
- How will you display your learning target for the day?
- What requirements does your school have in place for your pacing guide and/or curriculum?
- Are you able to hold one or two mini-lessons during your literacy block? If you are only able to hold one mini-lesson, will you need to have alternating days for teaching reading and writing?

5 | Pump Up the Jam, Pump It Up

During my transition from kindergarten to fourth grade, there was a massive explosion of classroom transformations that had taken over the online teacher community. Teachers were spending hours planning creative and engaging classroom designs that would transform their environment for one to five days. From Mario video game themes to safari jungle themes, teachers were taking a birthday party theme and placing it on steroids to engage their students. Did it work? Absolutely, it did; I know this because I was one of those teachers that drank the Kool-Aid that summer.

That first year in fourth grade was filled with mini-transformations (see Figure 5.1), such as a doctor theme where students would create a writing piece around a time they got hurt, to much larger transformations where the students were pirates trying to compete and find the treasure at the end of the day. The smaller transformations were always less stressful. I could make the room feel a little different by adding some music, giving students some themed props such as hats, glasses, or even clothing items such as gloves, lab coats, and more. With some quick and easy table covers from the Dollar Tree, I had a mini-room transformation in less than 20 minutes!

The larger transformations took much more time and energy to arrange. I'd like to do a quick shout out to my husband Trent for always helping me

Figure 5.1 Transformations from first year of teaching 4th grade.

through this process; teacher husbands are the best! I was always mindful of topics and themes that I thought my students would enjoy. That year I had several students who expressed their love for Minecraft early on. They brought in books to read and were constantly singing the Minecraft song during breaks in class. That spring, I put on a Minecraft Day where my students were taken through test-taking strategies (see Figure 5.2). They each received a Steve head to wear. They had different challenges, items to mine, and at the end, they had to defeat the evil Ender Dragon.

Figure 5.2 Minecraft Day.

I was so proud to give my students experiences that they would always remember. To this day, I still get students who email and tell me that they will always remember those days. I don't ever regret the choices I made in that first year because without them I would never have grown to the teacher I am today. The reality of those big transformations is that I would spend from 4:00 to 11:00 p.m. creating the transformation. This doesn't include the time I spent gathering materials, making activities, purchasing resources, and printing and cutting all the items needed for the day. I would spend anywhere from $150 to almost $300 for a single transformation. Yes, many of the items can be reused, and while I have yet to hold another Pirate Day, the items do come in handy during Halloween.

How is this sustainable? I can tell you that it's not. Thinking that you have to spend an insane amount of time and money for a single day during multiple points in the year can only wear on you physically and mentally. After that first year, my classroom transformations were few and far between. Now I am much more intentional with how I create an experience and engage my students in class. I've found that I don't have to spend money or hours, instead I just need to *show* them how to engage with the content. Engagement has changed from a bought-for-single-day event to authentic and rigorous opportunities.

Lessons Learned

The time that I spent growing the next few years taught me a lot about engagement. Some of these lessons I want to share with you. First, I learned that engagement can be a powerful tool to manage student behaviors. When students are engaged in their learning, then they are focused on the task at hand. Don't confuse this with entertaining your learners. Entertaining can spiral into a chaotic scene that will leave you pulling your hair out, and the initial objective of the class period forgotten. Understanding the differences between the two are critical to ensuring the success of your class period.

Second, engagement does not have to be a big production. Engagement can be created at a variety of levels, all of which will be introduced to you in this chapter. While the transformations that I shared at the beginning of this chapter are huge undertakings, they did engage and excite my students in the learning that was taking place. What I learned, however, is that there were other occasions when that same excitement was shown during much smaller learning activities. For instance, a simple game of Hedbanz with the timer countdown running to the tune of a James Bond film had my students going wild.

Another lesson that I was able to learn is that students need to be taught how to engage with content. We have a lot of competition. Almost every child has some form of a device at their fingertips; whether it is a cellphone, iPad, tablet, PlayStation, or any other electronic system, teachers have to compete with how these devices keep students' attention. I learned this lesson from my youngest son. When we first gave him an iPad, a pattern formed of him coming to us to download a free game. After some time, he would come to us again asking for a new game; after all, it was free! When we asked him why he wanted new games he told us that the ones he had were either too hard or boring. I was allowing him to give up and move on to something else. He didn't know how to engage with the content, especially when it got more difficult. Our classrooms are no different. We have to show students how to engage even when the content gets more challenging. How do we do this? We have to model this each and every day.

Finally, I learned that engagement needs to be about the learning and not the activity. Creating fun lessons is exciting for teachers, just as it is for students. The joy we feel when we have a new game for students to play or a transformation that we've spent hours designing re-energizes our love for teaching. However, it can be easy to get lost in the decorations or the excitement, and if we're not careful, the learning can be lost.

Engaging through Conversations

Conversations are the gateway to building relationships, acquiring knowledge, and fulfilling the need for human interaction; but conversations don't always come easy. I have always struggled with holding a conversation with others. My brain wanders; I struggle with how to move from one topic to another, and I often want to retreat to my hermit shell and hide. Others find conversation so seamless that it makes me green with envy. I've always wanted to be that person who could talk to anyone about anything and leave remembering every single detail.

Conversation can be an easy and effective method for creating an engaging environment. We know that students learn from one another, that perspectives give insight into alternative approaches, and that it is critical when teaching collaboration. However, we have to teach our students how to engage in conversations. If I would have had an opportunity to learn and practice holding conversations with others, then I might be more skillful at it as an adult. So how do we teach kids how to hold conversations? We scaffold it just like any other skill or strategy.

Ways to Scaffold Conversations

Scaffolding conversation should begin with the teacher modeling how to hold a conversation. This means teaching students the key elements that need to take place when having a conversation with others. If you hold a morning meeting, this is the perfect time to teach these components. Students should understand how to:

- Make eye contact.
- Focus on body language (leaning in, nodding, smiling, facing the speaker, etc.).
- How to respond to something they noticed or heard.
- Asking a follow-up question.
- How to disagree politely.
- How to add to someone else's thoughts.

Start small and practice with simple, non-academic, topics. This is why I mentioned teaching these concepts during morning meetings because it is a perfect and authentic time to have these conversations. Model how to hold conversation by asking for a volunteer and then acting out what it should look like. Then ask learners to make observations to share when you are finished. Do this several times at the beginning of the year before introducing these components during learning times. Remind students of the expectations for holding conversations when you are ready to incorporate more conversation and collaboration in your lessons. It might also be beneficial to utilize sentence stems that give your students a structure for their thoughts. Here are some ideas to get you started:

- I think ____ because ____.

- My opinion is ___ because ___.

- What makes you think ___?

- Can you explain ___?

- I agree/disagree with you because ____.

- I would like to add ___.

- That's a great idea. Another idea could be ____.

It might be helpful to have an anchor chart handy with the preceding elements for students to reference. To make this more meaningful, co-create the anchor chart with your students. You can add to your sentence stems throughout the year. Here are some simple ways to begin incorporating more conversations and collaboration in your lessons.

Discussion Questions. Create discussion questions for any text or topic that you are teaching in class. These need to be elevated and thought-provoking. Avoid yes-or-no questions with your students. Discussion questions can be specific to the events of a story, their thoughts on a meaning of a word, predictions, inferences, or it can be a way to inspire students to make connections. Some simple ideas would be asking if students would want to experience something that the character has, how they would respond to an event, or share stories that relate to the story in some capacity. You can even have multiple questions that students are required to move about the room to answer in small groups. Take time to prepare these in advance and decide whether your students will turn-and-talk or discuss with partners. The more thoughtful the questions are, the more engaged your students will be during your lesson.

Reteach. Giving students opportunities to become teachers can be incredibly powerful. Build in opportunities for students to turn and teach a concept that you are discussing in class. You might have students share the meaning and examples of a type of figurative language, share how they identified a character trait while reading, or how a certain type of text feature benefits the reader. The key here is that you will want to have explicitly shared the correct meaning and examples with students. Some helpful tips here are to give learners a role. You can assign them a letter or color so that students know who will talk first. After students turn and teach, invite one learner to share their explanation to the entire class.

Numbered Heads (see Figure 5.3). This simple activity can be reused for any type of text. Students will be in groups of four or you can accommodate and do groups of three by leaving out one of the role cards. You will have four roles in each group:

1. Read the question.
2. Answer the question with evidence to support.
3. State whether they agree or disagree and why.
4. Summarizes the question, answer, and evidence.

Each group will have a set of the role cards. Students will pull from the pile and start with the role they pulled. Groups will also have a second set of cards that contain questions that have already been created by the teacher. Students will keep these cards face-down in the center of the group. The learner with card no. 1 will pull from the pile of question cards and read the

Figure 5.3 Numbered heads activity.

question. Each student will then follow completing their part of the answer. Before pulling the next discussion question, students will rotate the role cards so that each one has a new role. Learners will repeat this until they have answered all the discussion questions or when time is up.

Snowball Discussions. This concept is a great way to get students to hear multiple perspectives around a discussion question. Begin by having your students in pairs and giving them ample time to discuss a question. All groups will answer the same question. After time is complete, the pairs will then join to form groups of four. Provide learners with some time to allow learners to share their ideas, and then ask groups to join and create a group of eight. The process continues until the entire class is engaged in the discussion. This activity is best used for questions that might contain some form of an opinion or require tremendous insight. For instance, in the short story "The Lottery" by Shirley Jackson, you might pose the question: *What form of symbolism is present in the story?* This will allow learners to come up with a variety of options because some students will share the box or the dot. Similarly, in the picture book *The Invisible Boy* by Trudy Ludwig, you might pose the question: *Why does the illustrator use some color in certain areas and black and white in other areas?*

Literature Circles. To increase more independence and higher-level thinking, incorporate opportunities for literature circles. These roles are ideally used in chapter book studies because students will have opportunities to complete multiple roles while reading the text, but can also be used for shorter texts. Students have a role that will get them to focus in one area while reading. For example, they might visualize and share their drawing, pick out vocabulary and share the meaning, or ask questions and discuss with their group. A set of literature circle cards are provided for you by visiting www.buildingtheliteracyblockresources.com. The key here is to limit the amount of work you give your students. The focus is on the discussion around the text. Many teachers will have one-page assignments for students to complete for their specific role. Save yourself the trouble of grading, and have students use sticky notes and place them in the book. This will also allow students to reference the page number while holding a conversation with their group.

Quick Tip: Before having students discuss the questions in groups, use some of the discussion questions as a whole class. Leave a few questions that are new and thought-provoking. This will help support students during the group discussion and give them opportunities to pull from the whole class discussion. It will minimize anxiety and support students in the learning process.

Socratic Seminar. This is a much more challenging form of discussion, but it is possible across multiple grade levels when modeled and prepared for properly. A Socratic Seminar is meant to be a student led discussion around a particular text or topic. Students are seated in a circle where they can see each of their peers. Students hold a discussion using guiding questions that were provided a few days prior. Students have had an opportunity to locate answers and find evidence prior to the day of the seminar. The teacher can sit in the circle and act as a guide to help prompt students to discuss when there is a lull in the conversation. Students share their thinking, make connections, and agree or disagree with their peers. This is a powerful method in a classroom, but does require some time for students to become comfortable with the process as it can be very intimidating. The teacher can call on certain students in the beginning to help encourage them to speak up.

Loving a Good Sort

Discussion questions and roles are not the only method to encourage collaboration and discussions. A great way to help scaffold instruction and use for planning meaningful and engaging activities for your mini-lessons are to incorporate sorts. This is one of my favorite go-to activities because there is a wide range of methods for getting students to discuss and collaborate with the content. To help establish the expectations for the activity, inform learners that they will have to equally divide the cards among all the members of the group. Students will take turns reading the cards and then allow for all members to share where they would place the card on the sort. When all the students in the group agree, the card can be placed down. This continues around the group until all the cards have been sorted. Here are a few of my favorite sorts.

Regular Sorts. This category refers to sorts that have a pair or set of headers in bold. Students will find the headers prior to beginning the sort. It may speed up the process to inform learners which header they need to look for and how many there will be. For added difficulty, you can remove the headers completely and have students determine the category through analysis of the cards. These sorts can include types of figurative language, character trait versus feelings, and sorting strong versus weak evidence from the text. A list of sort types is provided with the resources for this book. Organize these cards into Ziploc® bags or envelopes to help keep them secure to use them each year.

Sorts with Organizers. Another method for creating engaging sorts is to utilize a variety of organizers. This is a great way to scaffold graphic organizers for students. This will give learners an opportunity to see the content that needs to be included and can then mimic that during their independent work. Students follow the same process as with other sorts and share the responsibility of reading the cards and mutually agreeing where the card needs to be placed on the graphic organizer. Some ideas for this type of sort are a plot map, Venn Diagram, BME (beginning, middle, end) organizer, T-chart, and more.

Quick Tip: Use colored paper or numbers on the back of the sorts to easily organize. It never fails that one of your groups will leave out one or more cards to a set. In order to know where that card belongs, create easy-to-see differentiation by printing each group onto a different color of paper. If you don't have access to enough colors, you can use numbers or symbols on the back of each card in the set; you will also want to place it on the outside of the envelope for quick reference.

Sorts for High-Level Thinking. Sorts don't always have to be lower-level thinking. This sort will get students discussing the best option for how to respond to an open-ended question. Reading responses are a big component in upper elementary, and they are one of the most challenging to help students master. In this activity, find a concept that students are expected to write a response; for instance, theme, summarizing, and so on. Prior to the activity write out three to four different responses. One of the responses is correct and the others have some errors. For example, with summarizing, one of the incorrect responses will have dialogue inserted, the other might not have included a topic sentence, and finally, the last one might have been copied directly from the text. It is helpful to identify areas in which your class struggles so that you can address those in the beginning. Students work in their groups to read each of the four responses that are coded with a letter in the corner of the card. Groups decide which is the best response and should explain why. For added difficulty, remove the correct version and have students select one of the incorrect responses. Students must tell what is incorrect and discuss how they would write a proper response.

Methods for Pairing Your Students

The more you work with including conversations and collaboration into your lessons, the more you will find that certain students don't particularly mesh well. This has been the case in my own classroom. However, it is very important to teach students how to work collaboratively even though they might not be friends. Articulate to your students that no job will be mindful of who you are working with, and there will always be at least one person that you will struggle to like. Therefore, it is critical to go beyond the typical process of using popsicle sticks to name partners or even allowing students to choose. Create more fun by having some creative ways to partner/group your students. The focus will be removed from who they don't want to work with and instead be on how to find their partners. I only recommend using this method for short activities. Any long group work assignments should be thoughtfully planned based on their level by the teacher.

Sorting with Puzzles (see Figure 5.4). This is one of my favorite methods for sorting my students into random groups; so much so that I have two separate sets for building groups of four and sets or building groups of three. This is especially beneficial if you have an odd number of students in your class. For this partner sort, head online and find images of book covers that you enjoy or know that your students enjoy. Copy the image and place it onto a Google Doc or Slide. You will need to adjust the size of the image to be about the size of a standard index card. Print out the book covers, laminate, and cut them out. In order to create them into puzzles, cut odd shapes into the book cover, and create however many you need to form a whole book. For instance, I might take the printed book cover of *The Wild Robot* by Peter Brown and cut it into three oddly shaped pieces. Pass out the pieces and have students find their matching pairs/groups. When they have matched up, they will take a seat in a small circle around the room with their pieces combined on the floor. Collect the puzzles, paperclip each of the pieces together for each book, and place into a Ziploc® bag for future use.

Figure 5.4 Book puzzles.

Opposites Attract. This is a perfect sort for creating quick and easy pairs in your class. Check the resources for this book to grab a set for your classroom by visiting www.buildingtheliteracyblockresources.com. Print out the set of opposites attract sort cards. Hand out one to each of your students, but be mindful to include only the correct number needed for your class. If you need to have a group of three, print an extra of one card and inform students that there will be a group of three. Students will stand and use the language: "I have _____ do you have ___?" They are not allowed to show their cards until someone has answered "yes." Once they have found their match, they will take a seat next to their partner.

Deck of Cards. Some days require little effort and prep on your part, which is why having a deck of cards is a great way to sort students. For this sort, students can be placed in however many to create a group or pair. Think of how many you want to group together—you can group based on number or symbol, or create a more complex sort by having students look for the right color and number. Determine the number of students in class, and how many will be in a group. Identify the cards needed, and on the day of the sort, pass out each card. Students will find their groups and take a seat in a designated area.

Incorporating Movement

Students spend a large portion of their day seated at desks or on the floor. To get students to engage in the lesson and get their bodies moving, because no one wants to be seated for that long, incorporate opportunities to move. These can be simple ways to get them walking around while still engaging in the content you are teaching. However, be mindful that a few of these methods require you to have your behavior management nailed down. The more opportunities students have to move, the more likely you will have to address behaviors. If my time as a kindergarten teacher has taught me anything, it's the importance of being explicit with every move they make.

Gallery Walk. I utilize this activity at several points in the school year. While traditionally the activity involves students simply walking around and viewing each other's work in silence, I have added an additional component. Begin by creating questions on five to six pieces of large chart paper. You might have students consider the characters of a story, view the illustration on a particular page, or discuss other topics that you are teaching. Place each of the anchor charts around the room. Divide students into equal groups and have them stand at the chart paper. Give each group only one marker. Tell students that you are going to set a timer for one minute (you can find fun timers on YouTube that have music like this one at: bit.ly/1MINTIMER) and have students only discuss the answer as a group. After that one minute, get everyone's attention and then tell them they will have one minute to write. Start the timer again and let students write. You will then have students switch to the next poster and follow the same process until groups have had an opportunity at each poster. When done, learners can move about the room feely to look over everyone's responses.

Maître d'. If you like to incorporate music, this is the perfect activity! There are no resources needed for this activity, except for a list of questions that you will want students to discuss. Have music identified and ready; you will only need one song. Tell students to stand scattered around the room. Inform learners that as the music plays, they are to walk around the room slowly. When the music stops, the teacher will call out a table for a certain number of students. For instance, the teacher might say "Table for three" or "Table for five." Students are to then create a group of that many students with those around them. Talk to your students about not running around to find their friends and instead to make a group using the people closest to them; the point is that they will have a mixture of students each time. Once groups are formed, give the question and allow students to discuss. Play the music and students will move around once again. Students will create a new group based on the table number the teacher calls out, and either discuss the same question or a new one. Repeat until you feel as though students have had an opportunity to hear multiple perspectives.

Hand Movements. This movement is independent, but is a great way to ensure students are paying attention. Create movements to represent various skills in your teaching. To help spark some ideas, you can visit the resources for this book to see a video of ones that I have utilized in my class. When you say a specific word or phrase while teaching, students are expected to repeat the word and complete the movement. This increases their awareness of the lesson and gets them to make connections in a different way. For example, when teaching plot to fourth graders, I would have students recite the elements of plot while making the plot mountain using their arms and hands. This made sure they each knew and understood the elements before having to identify them in a text.

Games for Days

Over my years of having my own boys at home, I have developed a love for card games and board games. In fact, we have an entire cabinet and a closet filled with just about any game that you can imagine. It never ceases to amaze me how engaged my own boys are when we play these games that I started looking for ways to incorporate them into my classroom. While these forms of activities are more challenging to prepare for, they do offer an incredibly high reward. Students are engaged and working to learn the content. If you are new to incorporating games into your classroom, identify one or two games that you would like to try and begin there for the year. The more you feel comfortable and grow in this area, the more you can add later.

Jenga (see Figure 5.5). Popular with educators, this is a great way to tackle a variety of concepts in literacy instruction. Purchase colorful Jenga sets, or

Figure 5.5 Jenga game.

you can buy mini Jenga sets from Dollar Tree and use paint markers to paint the ends of each block. Have students work in groups of three or four and provide each group with a list of questions for each color, and a recording sheet for each student. You will want a total of 45 blocks and create equals sets of five different colors. This means that you will have nine blocks for each of your five colors. Using a simple template, write a variety of questions. Each color can represent a category, or you can create more challenging questions for each color. Students will take turns pulling a block and placing it on top. As a student pulls a block, they will answer the questions in order for that color. So, if Student A pulls a pink, then everyone in the group will answer pink question no. 1. If Student B then pulls another pink, everyone will answer pink question no. 2. The beauty of this game is that it leaves no one out. Continue until time is up or students have completed the questions.

Spoons. This activity is great for grammar concepts, such as identifying synonyms or antonyms. Create a deck of cards for each group. The cards will include four to five groups that each make up four of a kind. For instance, you might have four verb cards, four noun cards, four adjective cards, and so on. Print these onto cardstock or use labels to adhere to a real deck of cards for ease of use. Students will be placed into groups of four or five, and one student will shuffle the deck and pass out four cards, faced with the words down, to each player. In the center of the group, there is one less spoon for the total number of players. For instance, if there are four players, you will have three spoons, and so on. The dealer will pull a card from the pile and remove one card and pass it to the player next to them. Each player will pass a card until someone has found four of a kind. When this happens the player with four of a kind will grab a spoon and all players will race to capture the spoons in the middle. The player who does not get a spoon is out. To keep all students involved, have students maintain points. The person who grabs the spoon first gets two points, and everyone else that is able to capture the spoon gets one point. You can even add a point value to the spoons to make it even more competitive. Instead of the last person sitting out, the game would continue.

Bingo. Everyone loves a good game of Bingo! In this activity, have a board for creating various types of bingo cards. You can even have students make their own cards by supplying a list of words, concepts, or characters/objects from a book you've been reading and have them fill their own card templates. Use simple cut-out pieces of paper for markers and hold Bingo during a class period. This is perfect for sub days, review for tests, or a simple break from normal activities. Have prizes to hand out as learners win!

Jeopardy. There is no creating for this resource because teachers from all over have spent time making and sharing premade jeopardy templates online. You can check out the abundance of game boards over at jeopardylabs.com. A quick twist is to have students work in groups to compete against one another, or you can do this whole group by having a set of index cards with a students' name written on each one. Pull a card and have the student select the category and amount. All groups and students are expected to participate. If the student who selected the category gets the answer correct, they get to double the point value. All other students that got the answer correct will get to take the amount value listed. Students that did not get it correct receive no points. Learners can use a whiteboard to show answers and keep track of points. Add some "Jeopardy" music in the background for added fun.

Headbands (see Figure 5.6). This activity is perfect for reviewing characters, places, and objects from books. One of my favorite examples is the book *The Miraculous Journey of Edward Tulane* by Kate DiCamillo. On index cards or using a template you've created in Docs or Slides, write the names of objects and characters from a text, or have it based on a concept students are learning in grammar. Students are placed into pairs and given a deck of cards and an elastic headband. Students decide who will go first, and this learner will place the headband around the back and to the front of their forehead. The deck of cards is then placed behind the headband so that the student facing the player can read the card. The player reading the cards will give hints to help their partner identify the word. If the player gets it correct, they remove the card and place it in one pile. If they get it incorrect, they

Figure 5.6 Headbands game.

place the card in a separate pile. The teacher can create added engagement by incorporating music and a timer for students. The number of cards correct is the total points awarded. The deck is shuffled, and partner roles are swapped.

Buzzers. Colorful buzzers can bring excitement to any simple discussion and question activity. These can be purchased online in sets of four. For more groups with fewer students, consider purchasing two sets. Place students into groups with a buzzer at the center. Create a PowerPoint that will reveal the question or you can simply read aloud the question to students. The group that buzzes first and has the correct answer wins a point. If the group that buzzes first gets the answer wrong, then it is open to other groups to try and steal the point. Make this more fun by having bandanas in different colors to hand out to groups and allow each group to create a team name. This will create community and add to the competitiveness.

Mini-Transformations

While I may not hold many transformation days in my classroom anymore, there is still something to be said about adding a little bit of flair to create a special experience. This section offers some simple ways I've added flair for a low-cost and quick assembly. These are mini-transformations that I do each year to create some mystery to my classroom environment.

Theme Days. These are especially beneficial toward the end of the year, but theme days, as the name suggests, revolve around a theme. I've done a sea theme, pirate theme (that wasn't so over the top), golf theme, and more. Other teachers have done glow days or days revolved around a game or time of the year. The possibilities are endless. However, if you are like me and time is limited, don't be afraid to get your students involved in the creation process. Have students help decorate and build up the anticipation of the experience. Once you have a theme, you can create lessons around this. In order to help guide you in the process, I have included a theme planner to keep track of your lessons. You can choose how long to keep this up, but I would recommend no more than four to five days.

Mock Trials. Having to justify their thinking and cite evidence is an essential skill in upper elementary. Therefore, mock trials are a great way to build engagement, especially since these skills are the most difficult for students to master. To set this up, place a table or group of desks front and center of your classroom. You can use black table covers for simple decor. Place 10–12 chairs on one side and have two tables to make up the prosecution and defense. I use my old graduation gown for my judge robe, and give each juror a folder and pencil to take notes. This does require some prep, but it incorporates all the skills necessary to give a compelling argument. Hold court for a day, and you can either have teams switch to allow them to argue or hold a class discussion.

Book Tastings. These are my favorite days and so simple to make. For resources, collect red table covers or find inexpensive red and white checkered covers, red plastic plates, and make some simple chef's hats using white sentence strips and white tissue paper. Add some café music in the background and have students taste a variety of books by rotating tables and following a list of things to read. I will often have students reflect on the book cover, read the back of the book, and read the first four pages inside. They give the book a rating and move on to the next group. This is perfect for getting students to try books for a group book study or to get them interested in a book genre. You can have students vote by giving them three to four slices of paper to write their name and put them into baskets of their top three choices. Pull names to create easy and quick book selection and excitement!

Puzzles and Escapes. Puzzles and escapes offer students another element of having to collaborate and think critically about the resources provided. There are so many options for students, from online digital versions to elaborate escapes with clues hidden around the room. If you are a beginner to these types of activities, it may be beneficial to do one as an entire class. You can have students placed into pods at tables. Reveal the first problem and give groups time to solve it. Discuss how it was solved and move on to the next clue. This allows you to move about the room focusing on only one problem versus multiple problems. As students become more comfortable, have them work at their own pace in collaborative groups. It may also be helpful to have a set of questions or hints to give groups. They will get frustrated and want to quit; your role is to help support them so that they can push through and persevere.

Chapter Wrap-Up

Engagement comes in all different shapes and sizes. When you are intentional with your choice and make the time to model this for students, you will have a higher success rate of engaging your students in meaningful conversation. However, kids are still kids, and they will get off task. Find ways to help reel them back in without making them feel like they were wrong. Let's be honest, teachers can't even stay focused for extended periods of time. As a final thought, don't feel pressured to do all these activities that I have shared in this chapter or think that you can only use it once for the entire year. Rinse and repeat as often as possible. The more you use the activities, the better your students will understand the process and stop focusing on how to play. The focus then turns to what they are learning. That is when the real magic begins. Go slowly, know you will have to repeat and model, and don't be afraid to use it again. After reading this chapter, consider the following questions to guide you in implementing the new learning:

- Choose at least three to four activities that you want to try out in your classroom.
- Identify at least two to three concepts to use for each activity.
- Create the resources and have them stored ready for use when you have the activity.

6 | Say My Name, Say My Name

One of the biggest a-ha moments of my career came during the beginning of one school year. I had recently done some reflection of my literacy block and how I could potentially improve instruction in upper elementary. I had just completed my first year as a fourth-grade teacher, and at that time, I had taken on an even greater challenge of becoming a multiage teacher for fourth- through sixth-grade learners. I had incorporated data binders and student conferences in kindergarten, and since I had a year at the new school under my belt, I felt it was only appropriate to begin embedding elements that I was passionate about back into my teaching.

We were just beginning the lessons for launching our literacy workshop. I had given students a mini-lesson on building stamina during independent reading. We had already discussed just-right books, selecting texts from the library, and each student was equipped with a book that would pique their interest. I had my students fan about the room and find a just-right spot to continue building stamina. For the previous two days, I had taken notes and made observations of students as readers, and on this day, I was ready to start meeting with students one-on-one about what they were reading. This first meeting was something very simple and generic. I wanted to get to know their personalities and learn the topics that interested them.

All my fourth, fifth and sixth graders (I had around 25 students in this class) were seated around the classroom reading away. I grabbed my clipboard and found my first student. As I sat down on the floor next to this student, she turned and looked at me puzzled. I asked what she was reading and why she selected this book. The entire time I had the feeling that she didn't quite understand why I was talking to her. I then asked what her interests were outside of school. Again, a look of misunderstanding as she gave me short answers. This didn't seem terribly odd, as some students are apprehensive when it comes to talking to adults.

I moved on to the next learner and followed the same process. This student had the same reaction as the last. I received limited responses, confused looks, and apprehension. The next three students were no different, and I started questioning my approach. After reflecting for some time, I realized that so many of my students reacted the way that they did because they lacked the experience of having conversations about books, and depending on their previous teachers, they may not have had a teacher who had conversations with them one-on-one. Despite the practice of conferring being widely known, many teachers find the process intimidating.

I wanted students to be willing and excited to share their learning with not only me, but also with their peers, adults, and their families. I wanted students to be excited to come back to my table area and share their amazing growth, not turn around and ask, "Did she say my name?" as if they believed that they were in trouble. I held a meeting to discuss something that I would be implementing this year: conferences. I explained that I wanted to support them in their learning and that we would be meeting regularly so that I could work with them independently.

My first experiences with student conferences with this class was like the first time I sat with them during independent reading. They didn't know how to share their learning. As time went on, I gave explicit instruction and implemented a variety of conference types to help structure this time. Sitting down and asking, "How are you doing?" just wasn't going to cut it. That year, I saw my students go from timid and closed-in to learners that openly shared where they were in their journey and that celebrated others' accomplishments.

Student Conferences

My time in education has taught me that teachers struggle most with establishing a routine for student conferences. It seems many whom I have met don't even have the knowledge and quite possibly the desire to meet with students independently. Why is that? Think to yourself for a moment. Reflect on your own practices in the classroom and on a scale of 1–10 (1 being "I have no idea what they are" to 10 being "I am a master at running conferences"). Where do you land? If you are on the lower end of the scale, is it because you've never received the support and professional development from your school? Are you hesitant due to student behaviors? Are you stretched with time and unsure where to fit it all in? I will tell you that some conferences are better than no conferences at all. The goal is to feel comfortable enough to get started and realize the impact that you are making.

Let's break down this idea of student conferences. A conference is a one-on-one meeting between a student and a teacher where there is a defined, purposeful discussion around where they are in their learning. This conference is meant to last no more than five minutes and gives the teacher insight into the metacognition (how the student thinks) regarding a specific area of their learning. Students share insights into what they think is needed to grow in an area, and the teacher offers support with additional resources, quick modeling, or follow-up with additional assignments or small group instruction. This process of conferences is then repeated to review the progress and continuously set new goals.

Conferences are a personalized approach to ensuring the teacher is targeting areas that each student explicitly needs in order to grow. One-on-one time is rewarding and it's important to take the time and truly understand the impact that it will have on your students. If you are able to grasp the importance of individual conferences, then maybe you will begin to look for ways to incorporate them into your daily routine. The first impact that conferences have on your students is it helps to build a student's understanding around the importance of learning. One of the biggest components in upper elementary classrooms is getting students to feel a sense of ownership and understanding of where they fall in their learning. This can be especially difficult if your school sends out grade-based report cards.

In my experience, few students come into a classroom with a desire to do incredibly well because they want good scores on their report cards. Most of my students don't start making connections until it is announced that report cards are going to be released to families the next day. The connection between what is happening, and their progress and achievement is lost. Individual conferences allow the teacher to articulate where they are in their learning throughout the year. This is something simple that can be achieved by having a student data binder or folder that contains a collection of their testing scores, and graphs to show growth or a drop in achievement (see Figure 6.1).

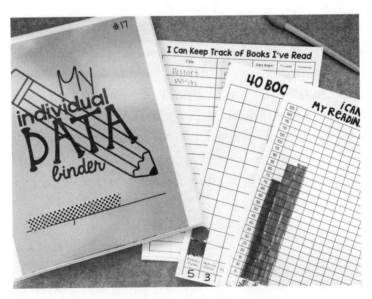

Figure 6.1 Data binder with graphs of achievement.

Conferences also hold students accountable for their learning. Many teachers ask me: *"How do you know when your students are reading, let alone comprehending what they read independently?"* The answer is having conversations with them and holding them accountable by asking those questions. Let's face it, when students fill out those responses to what they read, deep down they recognize it as busy work. Instead of adding more work on their plates and creating a pile of papers that you need to review and grade, hold a conference. You will, very quickly, recognize whether your students are on task. These conferences will also hold them accountable when completing work, revising, and following through with goals they have created. When kids have to sit down and explain themselves, they get uncomfortable. So, address the issues and help guide them with making good choices.

Every classroom has an array of needs; some struggle with reading; others can't comprehend, and many need guidance in their writing. We often have to teach multiple grade levels in one. Realistically, you cannot hold multiple lessons for each of your students, nor can you ignore the fact that all students need grade-level exposure. In order to create those modifications and offer support, individual conferences are ideal. Through the use of conferences, students can receive additional teacher-led modeled lessons, and support materials. Keep in mind that conferences don't just meet the needs of students below grade level, they can also be utilized to challenge students who are exceeding expectations during regular lessons. This is the element that establishes one component of individualizing the learning of your students.

Finally, individual conferences show your students that you care about their needs and where they are as learners. Remember Chapter 3 where we talk about building independence in our students? I mention that a big piece to creating independence is to show students that you care; there is nothing more special than sitting down one-on-one with a student to talk about them, to praise them, and to support them in their learning. Your students need to know that there is a reason behind what they are doing. Some will struggle to see the value for themselves, and others may not have the support at home. Be that person who helps them see their worth.

From Macro to Micro

One of my favorite activities as a teacher was during my first year at my second school. My principal held a meeting and told us all that we would be participating in a fishbowl activity. If you've never heard of a fishbowl activity, this is another great option that you can incorporate to build discussion and have students model various strategies and skills. For this specific situation, my principal divided us up into teams of teachers. Each group had a particular schedule where we would go around to other teachers in the building and be able to observe how they were implementing a specific area; in my case, I would be observing literacy blocks since that was my focus. I loved being able to see what others were doing in their classrooms and being able to take back small pieces so that I could grow as a teacher.

We learn best from one another, and even more so when we have opportunities to peek behind the curtain and see it all in action. While I can't have you come to my classroom, I can give you a macro (large) to micro (small) view of what individual conferences looked like. Starting with the macro view, this is a larger picture of all the moving parts that are taking place while I am pulling conferences. The biggest question teachers have is: *"What are the other students doing while you pull conferences?"* Since I am not a fan of literacy centers in upper elementary, I have students who are working on their independent assignment from their mini-lesson, working on goal work to share during their conferences, or simply reading. Now it is important to note that I don't start pulling all my conferences immediately after the first week of school. This is something that we build up to with modeling, discussions, and constant feedback that is being given during those first few weeks of school.

Depending on the events of the day, I begin class as I do most days. This includes our warm-up, open meeting, and mini-lesson. If I need to pull groups, then I take the time to do so. There are some days, however, where I find that my time is better served meeting with students individually than pulling groups. Use your best judgment with what your students need.

Check in with your administration and voice your thoughts on how individual conferences may benefit students when pulled regularly. If I had to pull groups, I would start with my intervention groups. On a typical day, I reserved about 15 minutes after the end of class (not including the close meeting) to pull a few students.

It took some time for students to know the routine for attending their conference, but as I would call students to come back to my area, they would bring their independent reading book, a data binder, pencil, and current work. We discussed their progress during the five minutes we had together, and if you are wondering, no, I did not have a timer running. I believe that timers can only cause more harm than good. It demeans the time with the student, and it causes you to think more about the time rather than the student. My recommendation is to look at your clock ahead of time and then again when you are done. Determine how much time you spent and reflect on why this happened. You'll find that you will improve naturally just by doing this trick than by having an external device dictate your time for you.

I begin by asking what they are working on currently. I have my recording sheet ready and my planner out for gathering any items on my list to follow up with or gather afterward. Once we discuss their work, I ask questions that are on my conference page. I have two options to choose from, and I'll share more of that in a bit. If I see an area of focus that the student needs additional support in, I might model the strategy and have the student copy my model right there. To end the conference, I take out the goal sheet from their data binder, and we review and discuss the present goals on the sheet. If the student met the goals, we cross that one off and determine new goals.

Keep in mind that many of the forms, goal sheets, and data binders are always accessible to students. This allows them to learn how to take responsibility and look at what they need to accomplish when they have extra time during class. After we create new goals, if needed, we discuss the actionable strategies and steps that the student needs to take. For example, if the student wants to incorporate other genres into their independent reading time, they might begin by reading a historical fiction by the end of next week. By breaking down the goal even further, it takes away the friction to get the student started on meeting that goal.

Types of Individual Conferences

We've looked at a larger picture of how conferences run within my own classroom, but now it's time to zoom in and get a better idea of how to make them work. To begin, we need to understand the differences between the types of conferences. These are important because as teachers it can be easy to see multiple areas that a student needs to improve on and want to target them all; however, we know that this strategy is ineffective and will only cause stress for your student and you. Therefore, we approach conferences with either an informal or a formal perspective.

In an informal conference you don't necessarily have a specific area of focus, and you simply want to hear more from the students on where they are in their reading and writing. Here are some guiding questions that I will tend to ask when holding this form of a conference:

Informal Reading Conference

- Show me what book you are currently reading.
- Why did you choose this book?
- Tell me about the book so far?
- Read this part of the book to me.
- Tell me about what you just read.
- Discuss strengths and weaknesses.

Informal Writing Conference

- What is your writing about?
- How and why did you choose this story/topic?

- Which part of this writing is your favorite?
- Discuss strengths and weaknesses.
- Give a teaching point and goal.

Notice these conferences are all about the work that the learner is doing independently. This does not pertain to a lesson, skill, or strategy that you have taught previously. Instead, it is about observing how the student interacts with the material with independent content. It also allows the teacher to gain insight into whether the student is implementing strategies and skills that they have previously learned, and what unassessed areas are of need to the student. The data collected from simple and informal conversations can sometimes be the most rewarding. These give you a deeper understanding of the students' metacognition, and what other areas may need to be addressed outside of your lessons.

In a formal conference, everything is more intentional and strategic. Normally, teachers have a specific area to address with students based on former observations through whole-group learning, small groups, or submitted assignments. As the teacher, start with identifying a point of reference. As mentioned, this might be an extension of a previous lesson, or it could be based on the individual's progression of needs. Feedback can be time-consuming from a teacher's lens, and even then, students might struggle to decipher ways in which they can improve their work. This might be due to students not understanding the material and need further guidance. A simple message on feedback can tell what they did wrong, but it may not help them figure out how to make the correction. Through a formal conference a teacher can explicitly walk a learner through the assignment, pinpointing areas of strength and weakness. At the end, the teacher models a different strategy that can then be placed into specific practice by the student. When devising this type of conference, there are a few elements that you will want to include:

- **Purpose:** Know exactly what you are going to discuss in this conference. This can be graded assignments, small-group lessons, whole-group observation, or a specific request from the student.

- **Compliment:** Begin by offering what you notice the student does well. Have this prepped in advance so that it flows naturally.
- **Teaching Point:** Discuss where the student can grow, and offer a quick teaching point such as a strategy or organizer for them to use.
- **Learner Implements:** Allow the student to model quickly and offer them feedback.
- **Goal:** Create a goal with the student so that they know exactly where/how to get started.

While the informal conference allows observations of how the student carries over their learning to more self-selected materials, the formal conference is about offering additional support in key areas of instruction. This is where differentiation and personalization occurs during your lesson. While it is not the only format of customizing the learning experience, it does play an important role. Students begin to develop more confidence and show a greater awareness of where they are as learners. It creates open lines of communication of where they are academically, without the added pressure of comparing themselves to their peers.

The Age-Old Question: Where has the time gone?

Time is a forever constraint and discussion in the world of education. We share students with intervention teachers, specialists, extracurricular activities, and teacher partners. How many times have you caught yourself saying, "Well, if only I had more time." At this point, you might understand the importance of individual conferences but you might be looking at your schedule and cannot begin to imagine how to make it all fit. I may not be able to give you the gift of time, but I can help you look, realistically, at how to implement conferences in your classroom.

Remember in Chapter 1 when I mentioned that I tend to have the *"Go Big or Go Home"* personality? When I first began conferences, I felt as though I needed to begin pulling all my students each week for conferences.

I prepped all my materials, had it scheduled using a calendar in my planning binder, and felt ready to tackle them. What could possibly go wrong? On Monday, I started with my schedule, and everything went according to plan. I felt confident about the remainder of the week, but as you can imagine, everything started to unravel. I dealt with behaviors, students were absent, I went over on my time, and wasn't able to meet with all my students that week. I felt defeated.

After that experience, I simply placed the idea of individual conferences off to the side. I didn't think that I was good at them and thought I just didn't have the time. It took many months before I decided to try again, and after that second try, I failed again. A year later, I realized that it wasn't my methods or understanding of how to incorporate conferences into my classroom that was causing me to fail; it was the fact that I was placing unreasonable expectations on to myself. Learning something new takes time. You don't just wake up one morning and say that you are going to run a marathon, you have to gradually work up to that point.

Big goals are great but you need to plan them through a scaffolded approach. Start with easing yourself into conferencing and build the number of times you pull students as you become more comfortable. As you move through the process slowly, you'll begin picking up ideas, and making changes that will fit your style of teaching. Plus, it will allow you to get your timing down early on. The first month that you want to start conferences, make a commitment to pull each student in your class once. This means that every day, your focus is to meet with one student. It doesn't seem like much, but I can assure you that it will feel like a change.

Next month, make the goal bigger. Instead of pulling all your students once in the month, make the goal to pull all your students during the next three weeks. Notice that I didn't have you pull your students twice within that month. This is because that can still be too overwhelming for you in the beginning. Slow progress is still progress. Once you are able to meet with each of your students in that three-week span, you can continue shortening the timeframe until you find the perfect amount. Meeting with all your students once a week may not be feasible for your schedule, and for other teachers, they might have plenty of time. Don't compare yourself to what other teachers are doing. Your schedule, the amount of time you have dedicated to your block, and the expectations you have will vary to other educators.

If you are working through the process, and you find that you are unable to meet a goal, then you need to take some time and reevaluate. Do not increase the number of times you meet with students until you feel confident with the process. This is key to successful student conferences. Ask yourself questions such as:

- Did I have a plan for pulling conferences?
- Did I have materials ready?
- Were my students prepared for me to pull them?
- Did I have circumstances that were out of my control arise (illness, assemblies, behaviors, etc.)?

Based on your answers to these questions, you might need to make some changes before diving back into the process. Reflection is essential when determining how you can improve. Looking for solutions will be the determining factor to your commitment in making this work. It took me years of practice, reflecting, and adapting to finally find a rhythm that worked best for me and my students.

Tips for Success

While I am far from being perfect, there are many things that I have learned and implemented that have allowed me to feel successful with student conferences. The first is to have a basic calendar or checklist available for checking students off your list. As much as you think that you can plan which students you will meet with on certain days, it isn't possible. Between illnesses, intervention teachers, and other pullouts, students are never there when you need them the most. The moment you try and place a student's name on the calendar, and they are not there, you will be completely thrown off. This means that you need to have a general idea of the next group of students you will be pulling. For instance, you can have students grouped into different colors. Follow the colors as you move through the conferences. For example, let's say you begin with the purple group for each conference rotation (the length of time you spend meeting with all your students). In the pull group are four students. You prepare the materials and purpose for each of the four students. Once your class begins, you can determine which student you will start with within that group. Once you get down to one student left, begin planning your conferences for the next group, and repeat until you have met with all your students (see Figure 6.2).

Next, determine how to communicate whom you will be meeting with for conferences. One approach is to simply announce the student(s) during your opening meeting or have it posted on your board as students arrive. Whatever you decide, be consistent. This gives students time to gather any materials or complete specific assignments prior to your meeting. It will ultimately keep the conference on task and running smoothly. Along with notifying students of their conference, it is important to communicate what they need to bring with them. For instance, you might have on the board for students to bring their folders, a pencil, and their independent reading book. You can choose to make this a routine, or have it posted in your classroom for students to reference.

I prefer to use conference tickets when informing learners of their conference day (see Figure 6.3). This is a template in the shape of a ticket, and it has key information. I make these in advance and pass them out to learners as they enter my class or have them placed on their desks. On the ticket is the student's name, the purpose of the conference, and the materials they will need to bring with them to the meeting. Notice that I don't add the date or time added, and this is because I have had too many instances where the date or time simply does not work. Keeping it open allows for more

Figure 6.2 Circle clip chart.

Figure 6.3 Conference ticket.

flexibility. As an added tip, use colored paper to print out your tickets. You can match the color of paper to the groups you have created to keep you organized.

Finally, once you begin the process of pulling students for conferences you will have an influx of students questioning when they will be pulled to meet with you. While this makes you feel incredibly special it can be frustrating when you are giving the same answer repeatedly. Have a system for sharing which colored groups students have been placed in, and post the color you are meeting with in your classroom. Think of it as a stoplight, but more colorful. As you begin your rotation, you can have a clothespin clip on the color you are currently on and the order in which you will pull the groups. For instance, you might have a purple color on the top, followed by blue, green, and orange. Also consider how to collect requests from your students. When your students realize the importance and benefit there is for meeting with you independently, they will begin requesting a conference to go over content they are struggling with. Have a box for students to add requests. You can have a set of index cards with a sign that asks for their name, the date, and the reason why they need to schedule a conference. When you have additional minutes, pull the index cards and begin addressing those needs.

Chapter Wrap-Up

Individual conferences can make a big impact on student independence and success. It builds community and trust between the teacher and student. Just remember that conferences do not have to be lengthy or time-consuming. Start small, build confidence, and go from there. As you work through Chapter 7, you'll begin to see the connection between individual conferences and how these relate to setting goals with your students. After reading this chapter, consider the following to guide you in implementing the new learning:

- Look at your schedule and decide when you will start pulling conferences.
- Choose a length of time to pull one class (meeting with all students once in a month is a great start).
- Determine how to notify your students that they have a conference.
- Determine what materials you need to have ready (page for notes, assignment materials to discuss, example strategies, etc.).

PART
3 | The More

One of the greatest privileges I ever had during my youth was being the youngest culinary manager in Darden Restaurant history. I was only 19, and while that seems very young to be a manager, I will say that I had amazing examples in my mother and father. I worked under an amazing general manager who taught me how to make observations and think for myself. During one instance, we were doing a routine check of the facility. I had my chef coat, clipboard, and I was ready to jot notes as he told me what needed to be done. We came to an area, and he looked around completely silent. He turned and looked me dead in the eye and challenged me, "Tell me what's wrong." How was I supposed to know that? He was the one who was teaching me! Not wanting to disappoint, I surveyed the area and began naming off items that I saw needed attention. While I may not have pinpointed exactly what he wanted, he pushed me to think critically.

Nearly a decade later, I encountered someone else who challenged me. It was my first year of teaching, and I was taking over the position of a kindergarten teacher who was becoming our reading specialist for the school. She was amazing at teaching kinders, and I was so excited when she took it upon herself to mentor me and two other new kinder teachers that year. We met once a week after school to plan and prep materials for the following week. Our school started to undergo some changes, and while we had the Harcourt curriculum, we were told that it could be used as a resource versus sticking to it to fidelity. During one of our weekly sessions, she sat behind my small-group area and myself and the two other teachers sat across from her, books open and planners out. I was going through the pacing guide and referencing the materials, and I turned and asked her a question. Now in full transparency, I have no idea what I asked her, but she looked at us and said, "Well, what do you think?"

The greatest leaders are the ones who challenge us to stop depending on the direction of others and instead take risks and look for solutions ourselves. One of the solutions educators search for is the development of a curriculum in literacy education. If a direction is given on what and how you teach, does this make you a good teacher or are you simply following the lead of others? Whether you are for or against a curriculum, we can all come to consensus that teachers need resources in order to provide authentic instruction. No matter what curriculum you have, it will never meet the needs of all your students. Why? Curriculum is made with a one-size-fits-all format, meaning it is developed for the average student in any given grade level, and we know that our students come to us with all different skill sets. Between the variation in our students' abilities, and the limitations of fitting in all that we have to teach during a restricted timeframe. There is no curriculum in the world that will account for all of your needs. Just as my general manager and teacher mentor asked me to go beyond the expected, we have to fill in the gaps by thinking about what is missing.

Each year, we welcome a new group of students into our classrooms. They think differently, they have different interests, and require guidance in different forms. Knowing this, we still open the same resources that haven't changed or been updated in the past five years and expect for it to work perfectly for those students. We can look around and make critical observations and decide on what needs to change to make education better. I realized this early on, and it is due to the great leaders that I had the privilege to work with at various points in my life. While my Pinterest scrolls, Instagram likes, and tireless Google searches led me to some great individual activities, I searched for the elements that would create the perfect learning environment that addressed all my needs. Have I found it? The strategies in the next three chapters have transformed my classrooms over the years.

The components I share in the chapters that follow can be adapted to the needs of your students, and target areas where the standard curriculum falls short. Your teaching style and classroom will determine how you implement these strategies, and while I cannot promise that it will solve all your problems, they will completely change the way your students interact and engage with the content you are teaching. I spent years looking for the right combination and implementation, and it has led me to discover three important takeaways. (1) The best practices are authentic. Finding ways to integrate real books, real experiences, and real conversations is the best ingredient to learning. (2) I realized that the greatest reward comes through the simplest practices. Not every lesson or strategy you implement into your classroom requires you to take time away from your family. (3) I concluded that I, too, was learning, and therefore, I needed to be open to making changes.

I was once teaching a lesson to a student and he looked up at me and said, "It's so simple that it's complicated." Sometimes it takes an outsider to help see how such simple and real experiences can make the biggest impact. His comment is exactly what we tend to do with simple topics. We think about it over and over, looking for the tricks, that we take this concept, and we make it difficult in our heads. As you read these last three chapters, try not to complicate any of the strategies that I share. Keep things simple and be content knowing that sometimes the simplest things in life give us the greatest reward. So, as you read through these chapters just remember this is all about REAL. SIMPLE. LEARNING.

7 | You Can Go Your Own Way

The years in which I made the largest growth in my career were also some of the most challenging I had ever experienced. My time as a multiage teacher taught me about the importance of knowing standards, identifying the differences between what fourth-grade writing and fifth-grade writing looked like, and changed the way I organized and created meaningful lessons. I had every grade level and ability level all in one classroom, and this meant that I needed to make the content they were learning different for each student. I focused a lot of my attention on learning the needs of each of those students because then I would have areas that I could specifically target when helping them grow as readers and writers. I sat down and met with them for conferences, but when those students walked away from my table something needed to happen.

One of the greatest mistakes that I made, and other teachers make, is not following through and acting when we see needs arise in our students. However, expecting teachers to create individual lessons for each need a student has is unrealistic. This might be where literacy centers were born: a teacher's instinct to provide practice on skills in a much more organized and predictable pattern. It makes sense, and it is more realistic than other options out there. However, centers are not made for everyone. In fact, some will argue that these forms of centers are simply glorified worksheets that place more work on the teacher rather than the student.

So, let's deep dive into understanding centers completely before exploring alternatives in upper elementary. Many teachers utilize a rotation system in which students will move from one center to another, practicing previously taught skills. Each center or station will have students complete a task such as matching puzzles, listening to a text in order to answer questions, and practicing essential grammar skills. It seems completely authentic and practical as these are skills that have already been taught and are important for students to have consistent practice. The issue with these centers is not all students require the same tasks, and we've talked about the importance of engagement and ownership when maintaining students' behaviors. Centers are the same as boxed curriculums, a one-size-fits-all format.

Instead of assigning tasks to all your students, focus on providing additional opportunities to only those who need it. For instance, you might have a student who struggles with fluency, and during one of your informal conferences, you create a goal for your student to practice their fluency three times a week. This means that you need to print fluency passages for the student to practice and upload their audio recording prior to your next conference. Or maybe you have a student who struggles with determining themes. In this case, you might pull some task cards for the student to complete and for you to grade and go over the results during the next conference. Finally, you might have students who struggle with writing descriptive sentences. Having students create sentences using the syntax cards you purchased a few years ago (and never ended up using) is a phenomenal way to allow them to manipulate their sentences while also being intentional with adjectives.

After listening to these examples, there might be a few things running through your head. First, you're probably thinking that I have now added more work to your plate and that there is no possible way to do this. Second, you might be wondering how in the world to identify what each student needs, and finally, how to manage this chaos without losing your mind. This chapter will help you develop systems to structure a goal station and how to get started.

Difference between Good Goals and Bad Goals

I love the start of a new year. I'm talking about a new fiscal year, or even a new school year. I love the idea of starting fresh, getting new supplies, and setting goals to grow. It took me many years to understand the difference between effective and ineffective goals. I would always start the year off strong, and about three days later, I would fall into the same old trap of what I did in the past. I have the terrible habit of not drinking enough water. In fact, I consume Diet Coke® as if it had the same properties as a glass of water. Every year I'd tell myself that I was going to quit drinking Diet Coke® or at least incorporate more water into my daily intake, and every year I'd fall into my same habits. Can you relate? Each year I failed because I was too unrealistic with my goals. They were broad and didn't give me actionable steps to scaffold (there's that word again) the process of incorporating more water and less Diet Coke®.

Whether working to build new habits or helping a student grow in their learning, all goals need a specific criterion for them to be attainable. Not all goals are effective, and in order to understand how to create useful goals, you have to think about each part of a larger goal. Some will tell you that it's not smart to have a broad goal, I don't think there is any harm in knowing where you want to be so long as you properly break down the goal into measurable steps. For example, if I say that I want to plan my entire school year, that large goal is the result of smaller goals that are constructed around it. I've utilized the SMART goal method by George Doran, Arthur Miller, and James Cunningham in my classroom. Keep in mind that these might be overwhelming to students, and it may be beneficial to give students guidance when creating goals for themselves. Here is what each letter stands for in SMART:

- **Specific.** The goal needs to be specific enough that it removes any vagueness from the overarching task. An example of a goal that is too vague is stating that you will start to read more genres. The idea seems great, but it leaves a lot of room for interpretation. Does this mean that you will read one new genre in a month or three months? Instead, a specific goal is to say that you will read three historical fiction books this month.

- **Measurable.** You want to ensure that you have a way to measure the goal. Meaning, you can say "yup, I did that" or "no, I didn't get that done." For example, if a student is working toward understanding and writing similes and metaphors, you might have students complete some task cards or develop a presentation defining similes and metaphors with examples. Having the ability to measure the goals that you create will allow you to build this into your own assessment and determine when students are ready for new goals.

- **Attainable.** Above everything, goals need to be realistic. Creating a goal to read three books in a week is unrealistic and it will leave students feeling defeated. It is important to create goals that you know students will be capable of achieving. As you work with the student, be sure to consider extracurricular activities, pullouts, and other conflicts that might interfere with creating this goal.

- **Relevant.** Think about the end result. Does the goal work toward this? For example, if the student needs to work on vowel patterns, does the goal give the student explicit, measurable practice toward understanding vowel patterns? Asking yourself whether the goal is relevant will keep your students on track to grow in areas of need.

- **Time Sensitive.** Your goal needs to have a timeframe for when students are expected to achieve it. For example, if the goal is to practice their fluency three times, give a time-sensitive phrase at the end by stating the students will practice their fluency three times each week for the next two weeks. This increases the awareness of the goal and gives students a clear understanding of their next steps.

Start by giving students some say in their final goal. For example, having a fourth grader plan a goal with each of the five components in mind will feel overwhelming. I have students give input on the time they spend, and whether they believe it is attainable within that amount of time. Each of these will keep you focused on creating goals that yield results. Think about our literacy standards. Much of what we do as teachers is to provide students with a variety of strategies that will help them achieve the skill necessary to become a good reader and writer. Breaking down tasks into these smaller, realistic, and structured goals will give clarity to their independent time. This also answers every teacher's dreams of reducing the number of times students ask "What should I be doing?"

Getting Started with Goals

As with everything that we have discussed in this book so far, starting anything new requires knowledge and a whole lot of grace. Conferences are crucial in implementing goal setting (see Figure 7.1). Make sure that you've taken the time to read through and begin planning how you will implement conferences into your schedule this year. Your conferences will be the

Figure 7.1 Goal setting with students.

gateway to helping you create effective and meaningful goals with your students. Start small and increase the goals that you create with your students. I recommend never exceeding three learning goals during your literacy block. If you give students too many goals, they will become frustrated and overwhelmed. This will also look incredibly different depending on your students. Some will likely have a reading goal, a writing goal, and perhaps a fluency/word study goal. Make sure that the number of goals you create are attainable depending on the students' schedule, level of assistance needed from the teacher or paraprofessional, and their ability level.

Begin the year with setting goals that pertain to them as readers and writers. Find small goals that are not connected to a reading standard. One of my favorite goals to discuss, and I will often get students involved in brainstorming goals together as a class, is to decide how we can read more independently. Whether this be based around reading a specific genre, reading for a length of time, or completing their first chapter book, brainstorm a list of ideas and go through the process of setting the goal together, even before you've had the opportunity to start incorporating conferences. Goals without accountability, and acknowledgment are not goals; they become simple sentences written onto a forgotten piece of paper. Set an intention and let students know that you will check in during the first round of conferences in a couple of weeks.

Additionally, create a system for checking in with students as they work toward their goals. One method is to have a spreadsheet easily accessible where you can see which goals students are working on each week. You can also have a printable template that gives you the ability to write goals in and reference at the start of every class. Place stars near the name of students who need frequent check-ins. Nothing screams accountability more than a teacher calling out exactly what students should be working on throughout the week. Refrain from scheduling a follow-up conference with the student in your planner. It is inevitable that things will go wrong, and changes will have to be made to your schedule. If you have time during your class period, you can walk around and target the students who need the most assistance first. Ask simple questions such as: "How are your goals coming along?" or "Did you have any questions regarding X goal?" Your check-ins will help to hold students accountable.

Finally, decide how you plan on storing or displaying the goals of your students. I've mentioned data binders or even folders at various points throughout this book. During my early years of teaching when I had a much larger classroom, I had a binder with each student's name on the spine. These binders sat in the middle of the classroom near the students' workspace. When I moved schools, my room was much smaller and the idea of 45 binders for two blocks of literacy just didn't seem reasonable, so I switched to folders (see Figure 7.2). The data binders/folders acted as a collection of students' growth across a variety of skills within literacy instruction. This record contained every score, exemplar, and of course, their goal sheets that the student could use to reference throughout the class period. They were

Figure 7.2 Binder versus folders.

never allowed to take these home, but I gave them complete access. Why? It built independence and trust. While this might make some of you feel uneasy, remember that keeping everything hidden behind your desk or in a file cabinet benefits no one. The idea is to show kids that they can lead their own learning and grow.

Creating a Space for Goal Work

It's unrealistic to pass out individual materials each day for your students to complete their goals. Part of the frustrations that most teachers have with literacy centers is having to make consistent changes to the activities each week. The greatest benefit to the methods I share with you, is that there are little to no changes you need to make for maintaining this station. In the beginning, as you are creating this station, you will have a little more work, but after some time you will simply be able to maintain the space and revamp activities as needed. Many of the resources that you once used for your literacy centers, activities, or instructing lessons can be placed into your station.

Locate an area in the classroom that can handle several students in one space. You might want to have this located in an open area of the room or where you have shelf space to help organize the materials. Students should be able to access these materials at various points during your literacy block so you may want to ensure it won't distract others. Within this station, gather a variety of activities for students to access and use for meeting their goals. Materials can be broken down by the area of reading or by unit for ease of use and quick access. Here are some ideas of activities you can place in your goal station (see Figure 7.3):

- Task cards.
- Reading passages with questions.
- Fluency passage of various levels.

Figure 7.3 Goal station.

- Word work stations.
- Grammar activities.
- Games that have been previously played during lessons.
- Graphic organizers.
- Copies of anchor charts.
- Exemplars of specific skills.
- Activities for implementing skills in their independent reading.
- Activities for implementing skills in their independent writing.

You may be reading through this list and wonder how this is any different than literacy centers. The main difference is the ability to customize the activities based on the needs of students, and that you are not constantly having to switch out activities. This is great for students who need a refresher of previous lessons. The goal station gives students access to all sorts of materials throughout the year.

Storage Solutions and Maintaining the Space

Having a sustainable system for organizing and maintaining your goal work resources will keep you from having to constantly give attention to the space. The goal (see what I did there) is to have this space grow as the year progresses and for it to require little attention on your part. For this to happen, you will need to be mindful of how you organize the space and materials. For starters, decide how you will contain the materials. As previously mentioned, the location of your goal station should be central enough that all students have access to the materials throughout the class period. Having some shelf space and using file bins to organize the activities will make it easy for students to quickly pull materials without causing a distraction to their peers. Personally, I use black bins that can be organized by the unit or skill (see Figure 7.4).

Identify a way to accommodate a variety of materials that will stay organized as students are removing and placing them back in their designated location. Folders with a zipper are ideal. Simple file folders to hold sheets of paper are an economical option. If you have smaller materials that students

Figure 7.4 Black goal bins.

will need to complete the activity, simply take a quart-sized Ziploc® bag and open it up. Take one side of the bag, and at the top of the inside folder, staple the bag to the folder. You will be able to store materials in the bag and still close it, keeping all the materials neatly secured. If you do decide to go this route, I suggest using plastic folders as students will potentially rip the folders opening the Ziploc® bags from the inside of the folder.

Another suggestion for organizing the chaos is to have colored folders to differentiate the skills or units that you have created to maintain the materials (see Figure 7.5). This will ensure that students place the folders back in the correct location. If space allows, you can store the folders to a specific color, for example: green in one bin versus placing all the colors together. Students who are looking to find resources on fluency will easily be able to locate all the materials in one spot. As an added security, create a label system that will help to place materials that have been left out back in their assigned

Figure 7.5 Goal folders.

location. For instance, the characters bin contained folders that began with a *C*. Each folder was then broken down by the skill and given a number. Each of the materials included in the folder should also be labeled with all the information on the back. It is inevitable that materials will be left in your room, and this system will ensure everything goes back to where it goes versus making a mess on your desk.

If you are placing materials in which students will be recording answers, you can create a system for knowing when materials are low. A simple strategy is to create a class set of copies. On the fifth to last copy add a sticky note that gives directions for students to either place the folder on your desk or to place the sheet on your desk so that you can make copies and add it to the resource. These systems, while they may seem extensive in the beginning, will make maintaining the goal station much easier throughout the year.

Finally, take time at the beginning of the school year to model the expectations for how to use this station. If you don't plan on using the station right away at the beginning of the year, it may be smart to hold off and discuss the expectations when you are ready to get started. Here is a list of items that you should keep in mind when modeling how to use the space:

- How to grab resources from the bins.
- Where to go when working with the resources.
- What happens when you need a partner to play an activity.
- How to know what resources you need.
- How to place resources back in the correct bin.
- What happens if something gets left out of the folder.
- Where to put completed pages for grading.

Once you begin using the goal station, feel free to rediscuss the proper procedures for using the materials. I would also take the time at the end of each class to look through each area of my room before dismissing. If items were not put back correctly, all learners had to stay until the classroom was back in order.

To Grade or Not to Grade

Grading in upper elementary is always a hot topic. Determining whether you should grade each activity that your students complete is your decision; however, I would advise against this. In all honesty, your students should not be working on goal assignments every single day. This should be added as students have more time, or it can be used during catch-up days or morning work. If you are giving feedback to all students for their regular work and add on the goal work, you'd be swimming in grading every evening. Have students take pictures with their device or keep track of their goal practice in a specific folder. During the next conference meeting, sit down and quickly look over the assignment giving feedback and reevaluating the goal.

The important part of all of this is to not over-complicate it. The more moving parts, the harder it will be for you to maintain the system. I recommend having students work on their goal practice two to three times per week. If you trust students to self-assess, keep a binder filled with page protectors and organized in a similar system as your bins with answer keys. Keep this binder in a location close to your teaching area so that you can monitor students in the space. Allow students to grade their own work and share during their conference.

Chapter Wrap-Up

Hopefully after reading this chapter, you have identified a connection between holding individual conferences and establishing goal stations in your classroom. The two go together and offer a learning experience that is tailored to the diverse needs of your students. If you are still looking for additional resources to support students with their goals, I recommend *The Reading Strategies Book* and *The Writing Strategies Book* by Jennifer Serravallo. These books will help simplify activities by incorporating strategies into the learners' independent reading and writing time. You can even have students keep a journal and complete their thinking in their notebooks. Above all, use your gut to guide you with what your students need most. You know your students best, and finding simple activities to support what you are teaching in your lessons will still make a difference. Consider the following questions to guide you in implementing the new learning:

- How will you record the goals that you create with students and share it with them?
- Where will you locate your goal station?
- Which materials and labeling systems will you use to help organize?
- How will you collect and provide feedback to your student?

8 | Celebrate Good Times

The last year I taught sixth graders gave me some big lessons about how I use time in the classroom. Due to the multiage format that I taught at the time, I had the same cohort of students for three years. Every group of sixth graders made an impact on me because I built such a great relationship with them all; however, this group was something special. During their fifth year, we had restrictions at the school and our once mixed-aged classrooms had to stay separate into grade level classrooms. I just so happened to have the fifth graders that year, and when people are in challenging situations together, it tends to bring them closer. Going back to their final year with me, many of the restrictions we had were starting to lift and we were excited to move about and use some of the strategies that they remembered from fourth grade. I had tried to continue the same experiences in fifth grade, but it just wasn't the same.

We were wrapping up our informational writing unit, and time was starting to feel a little tight to complete everything before the end of the school year. I told my students that we needed to get started on the next unit, and they all looked at each other as if I were missing something incredibly important. One student raised her hand and said, "But what about our author day?" (see Figure 8.1). I looked down and told them that we just didn't have the time. I needed to get in some specific lessons before state testing. The next few moments were of the students negotiating how we could possibly make author's day happen. Finally, after seeing their excitement and passion for author's day, I agreed. As students were leaving, a group of girls who had written about cookies came to me and asked if they could bring in cookies

Figure 8.1 Author's day.

for author's day. I thought it was a great idea and would make the event a little more special.

Everything was ready and as students came in their faces lit up with excitement. They praised each other's work; they were completely immersed in each other's stories, and the snacks were particularly delicious. This day was about them celebrating who they were as writers. Other teachers and assistants walked into the classroom, and they were taken aback by the commitment these students had to their writing. At one point, I remember our learning support teacher looking up at me and telling me that this was amazing. It melted my heart and opened my eyes to what this day was really about.

I left school that day with lessons that would stick with me for the remainder of my teaching career. First, when given the opportunity and support throughout the year, students support one another in their learning. Was every single writing piece perfect? No. However, students didn't care, they simply wanted to read the work that they had poured the last three weeks into. Second, students learn from one another. When I realized that I was not the only provider of information and that my students had strategies that could benefit one another, my pedagogy as a teacher completely shifted. Finally, students love to celebrate, especially with food. While it might seem frivolous to some, they are celebrating their learning. This alone is worth the $12 I spent on popcorn.

Celebrations in your classroom do not need to revolve around special holidays or school-wide events, these can go far beyond the basic ideals and create a larger impact on your students. What does celebration look like to you? Initially, I pictured balloons, confetti, and a special occasion that warranted the attention of others. However, the more time I spent in the classroom, the greater my realization came to be that celebrations are about big and small moments. My first experience with creating special moments started when I realized the importance of celebrating the first day of school. We often have end-of-the-year parties where we are excited for summer and proud of the work we've done all year, but imagine a classroom that celebrates students entering the classroom for the first time. This sends the message that you are excited to have them there and you are looking forward to the upcoming school year.

Over time, as both a teacher and a mom, I have learned to enjoy the simple aspects of life. While there wasn't someone there throwing confetti around for these small moments, they were memories that I wanted to cherish. I wanted to show students how to love and be excited for what they accomplished in their own learning. I wanted to give them something to celebrate because it was worth a celebratory moment. This is when I began incorporating two key celebrations that we would have as a class throughout the school year. The first was celebrating the books we read through the use of book talks, and the second was celebrating us as writers by incorporating author's day.

The goal of this chapter is to give you actionable steps to making book talks and author's day a reality in your classroom. You'll learn about the purpose of each of these strategies so that you can communicate the importance with your students. You'll learn key steps to implementing these into your classroom, and how to organize the event and materials. The chapter concludes with ways to make this into more of a celebration and keep students engaged throughout the year. The hope is that you feel adequately prepared to take some aspect of these two components and see the impact that they can have on your student's self-worth and ability to create a positive classroom community.

Book Talks

Every literacy teacher wants to experience a group of students who love to talk about books. That sixth-grade class that I mentioned at the beginning of this chapter allowed me to see the possibilities of what a literacy rich classroom could look and sound like. They shared books, sought out new recommendations from peers and teachers, and they would even sucker me into giving them an entire class period to just read. Amazing, right? What you don't know is this group of students wasn't always like this. Yes, I had some who came to me with a passion for reading, but during their fourth-grade year, many of them were like every other group of students. They read when they had to, and just like every other group of students, I introduced them to the power and joy of book talks. This is where I believe their love for reading grew and spread into the hearts of other students in the class.

The premise of book talks is exactly what the name implies; it is an opportunity to have conversations around the books we are reading. It isn't like having a book club. In fact, this is incredibly informal and done after the student has already read the book. Book talks are quick presentations about a book in order to persuade others to read it. Through these simple and quick presentations, students develop skills that will benefit them in other areas. First, they work on their speaking skills. This process will give students more opportunities to stand up in front of their peers and get comfortable with the idea of talking to a large group. Second, students are held accountable for reading and sharing the book. Depending on your system, you will determine the number of book talks that students are expected to give each month. Finally, students develop communication skills. Being able to effectively communicate your thinking is important, and in order to grow, students need consistent practice with these experiences.

So, what does this look like in a classroom environment? This can vary with how you choose to implement but over the years, I have found the perfect method for my classroom. I've mentioned in previous chapters that my literacy block begins with a quick warm-up. After reviewing and giving feedback, I hold a short 5- to 10-minute meeting with the class in which we discuss expectations, and I remind students of the work they need to complete. Then I allow students to share their book talk with the class. This is scheduled using a simple calendar that I share later in this chapter, but I start by calling one student to the front. The learner will then proceed to stand up and present the book they are recommending to the class. While they speak, I sit out in the audience, in this case in an empty desk or a spot on the floor, and complete the rubric to share with the student later (see Figure 8.2). When the student is finished, we give a round of applause and I open the floor to questions or comments. After the questions have been answered we give one last applause before the student takes a seat. Seems simple, and that's because it is. Even though there isn't anything flashy or fancy, these small conversations allow us to celebrate the books we are reading as a class.

Types of Book Talks

Before getting started with book talks, you may want to familiarize yourself with the variations there are and look for creative ways to engage your students. There are four types of book talks that I have conducted in my classroom that will hopefully give you a starting off point. The first is your

Figure 8.2 Rubrics for book talks.

standard book talk. In this format, students are simply standing up in front of the class and reading off a script that they have completed a few days prior. Many students will bring in props to act out small scenes, or to create a simple display area for other students to look at during the class period. I encourage students to have a physical copy of the book to show their peers, and if this is a copy that I have in my classroom library, I often have it displayed for students to look at afterward.

The second type of book talk is a video format called a book trailer. Students use an application or online program to create a trailer that gives the audience an idea of the book without spoiling the ending. Depending on the technology that your students have, this might look very different in your own classroom. For my learners, they go through a paper planning process where they outline how they will structure their book trailer. They can use images, act out scenes, or for some of your more creative students, draw individual scenes and create a stop motion. They compile all of these into a book trailer template (iMovie comes with formats that are easy for students to drop in the media). Before sharing their book trailer with the class, I have students complete an introduction.

The third format is very similar to the standard book talk but requires an added element. This format is called a blog post, and is especially special if you have a classroom blog that you share with families. Students follow the same process as the standard book talk and complete a written book talk using a template provided by the teacher. When finished, they then write the book talk into a blog post style and are required to take some images of the text to promote. Students are still expected to stand in front of the class, but they will have their book talk posted onto a projector and simply read the post aloud. I will then add the post to our classroom weekly newsletter for other family members to read.

Finally, this is one that has been newly added, thanks to that special sixth-grade class. This is a simple presentation format using an application such as Google Slides. In this format, students follow the same guideline for discussing their books but incorporate other media formats throughout. They provide imagery to help visualize as they share their presentation, and in some cases, short video clips of various discussion points about the book. Students have enjoyed this because they were able to combine all the previous book talk formats into one.

Implementing Book Talks

Providing students with clear expectations and guidelines to follow is essential when getting started with book talks. Reading chapter books, especially in the younger grades, can be challenging to remember, and without a clear set of guidelines, students will ramble incessantly about parts of the book that may not be significant. Have a system for students to follow for crafting an effective book talk. There is an abundance of resources available online, but here are the key elements that I have utilized in my classroom:

- **Provide your reader with an opening statement.** This is something that will hook your reader's attention. It can be in the format of a question, a quote from the book, or describe a vivid scene.

- **Follow with a short summary of the text.** Students offer the reader a gist of the story line by sharing the main characters, the problem that is faced, and gives the reader a hint as to what happens at the end.

- **Give the reader your impression of the book.** Provide your thoughts on the book. Give a little information about why you did or did not enjoy it and tell whether you would recommend the book.

- **Offer some closing thoughts.** Leave your reader on the edge of their seat and wanting to read the book by asking a rhetorical question or by offering them a cliffhanger.

When you share this format, place the information onto an anchor chart for students to reference, or create a reference page or outline that students can use when writing their own book talks. To ease into this process and to ensure that it is successful, begin by teaching students about book talks at the beginning of the year. I typically spend four to five days discussing and giving students practice with book talks. On the first day, I model a book talk and we discuss each of the components. I also have a few book talks that I share with students of online examples or video clips from previous students. After showing the example, I read a picture book of my choosing, and together we complete a written version of my book talk. Did you pick up that this is the We Do portion of my modeling? For the You Do portion, I have students go out and listen to an audio recording of a short story or picture book depending on your resources, and have students complete their own book talks. I choose two to three students to present it to the class and offer feedback. This process allows me to ease students into the process of book talks before sending them out and expecting them to complete it independently.

Something else worth mentioning is that I only introduce the standard book talk format at the beginning of the year. This gives me time to provide feedback, make sure all students understand the format of a book talk, and it gives me a little bit of leverage of adding in some variation and excitement throughout the year. If you're like me and wondering when you will teach the other formats, I like to sprinkle these in around breaks when I am reluctant to start a new unit, or when I know that I have a change in my schedule and need a shorter lesson. The beauty of making sure all students can structure a basic book talk is that they will use this same format for all the other media types. This simply gives them more opportunities to add their own creativity.

Finally, as you begin to implement book talks, you'll want to determine how you organize the materials. In my classroom, I use a small portion of our whiteboard space (see Figure 8.3). I place three magnetic pockets from Lakeshore that kept stocked copies of all the organizers for the book talk

Figure 8.3 Book talk station.

formats. As students needed to plan their book talk, they grabbed the necessary organizer and then submitted it to my basket. In that same location, I had a one-page calendar for each of my blocks. Before posting for students, I would reference my calendar and cross off any days that I did not want my students to sign up. This could be due to half days, no school, or special events that would cause a schedule change. I informed students that only two names were allowed to take up each date, and students would freely pencil in their name. One or two days prior to that class I would reference the sheet and ensure I had checked over their book talk.

Establishing Expectations

Creating expectations is important. This levels the playing field, and it holds students accountable. My first expectation that I established was the number of times students were expected to present. When I initially began with book talks, I gave my students free reign of when they chose. This quickly turned into the same five students holding book talks every couple of weeks and never pushed other learners outside of their comfort zone. Somehow, I went to the opposite end of the spectrum and told students they had to complete two each month. As you can imagine, this was unrealistic. I had students overwhelmed, and I found tracking learners' progress too time-consuming. And then, in a Goldilocks sort of way, I found the spot that was just right. I switched to telling students they only had to complete one book talk a month. This was simple because I could place a class list next to the calendar. and as students would complete their book talk, they would cross it off the list. Be mindful of not crossing their names off when they initially sign up, there might be times when students have to reschedule because of weather or an illness. Crossing the name off as they finished ensured they followed through with the presentation. Students knew they had no other option to complete a book talk a month, and if you're wondering what I did with the learners who were reluctant, I sat down with them at the beginning of each month and had them decide on a date. I checked in on their book selection and when they submitted their book talk for review.

It's always funny how situations will cause new rules to be created or expectations to be established. I had one student who loved to read. In fact, her favorite genre of books was realistic fiction. One day she had a book talk that she was going to present. I hadn't looked over her book talk, but she was an exceptional student and I felt as though it would be fine. Little did I know the book she shared, which was not one from the school library, was filled with discussions about puberty and breast development. Laughter erupted from the class, and I could feel the heat in my cheeks. From that day forward, students were no longer to present their book talks without my approval. The expectation was for students to have their book talks submitted to me two days prior to their talk for me to review and approve. If I felt revisions needed to be made, they could resubmit the day before or change their book talk to the day after in order to give them more time.

One final expectation was during the book talk presentation. This process is not only about teaching students to communicate, present, and share a love for literature, but it is also about modeling how to be good listeners. During the presentation, students were expected to have their desks or tables cleared, and their attention fully on the presenter. At the end they knew the floor would be open to questions, and I always reminded students to listen to other questions so that we did not have repeats. My role was to take notes and complete a scoring rubric so that I could give feedback to the presenter at the end of class or during an individual conference. I always ended the presentation by complimenting something that the speaker did well and offered a way for them to improve. I did this in the presence of others because it was a learning experience for everyone. The more we normalize that none of us are perfect, the easier it is for us to receive criticism and grow from the experience.

Changing It Up

Incorporating moments of novelty and variation is a simple way to hook students back into repetitive tasks. It can be easy to lose excitement over sharing a book talk with your peers. In many cases, I have seen when students have tried to completely fly under the radar of not signing up or will share the same type of book, such as a book from the series *I Survived* or *Diary of a Wimpy Kid*. While there is nothing wrong with sharing books from the same series, it lacks variation. The point is to have students explore a variety of genres and topics that might be of interest and share the journey with their classmates. To help encourage these practices, here are a few ideas to keep book talks spicy in your classroom:

- **Draw for the spot.** Instead of having students sign up throughout the month, have a day where you draw names and allow students to select a date. The fun part is getting students to give a drumroll on their desks as I select a new popsicle stick. If you are picked early, then you get the option to choose the end of the month; those who are picked toward the end might get stuck with the beginning of the month.

- **Hold a book talk day.** Another great option, especially when you have a shorter month due to breaks, is to hold an entire book talk day! You'll need to plan these in advance to give students enough time to get prepared and for you to approve their organizers. On the day, simply draw names and have students present their book talks. It makes for a fun day for you and your students.

- **Share your own book talks.** Incorporate your own book talks throughout the year. This is a great time to include books that you've read and would like to share with the class, or simply share titles from your own classroom library as a book highlight.

- **Invite other adults in the building to come and share a book.** This is one idea that holds a special place in my heart. Encourage other staff such as bus drivers, custodians, office personnel, or other teachers to come in and share books that they have read. It's a great way to build community and to build relationships with other adults in the building.

Author's Day

No classroom celebration is complete without author's days. I first was introduced to an author chair when I taught kindergarten. At the end of each day, I would select two to four students who would bring their writing up and share it using the Hovercam, a device that projected a physical item to the smartboard. When I transitioned to teaching fourth grade, students worked on a single writing piece for days, sometimes weeks, and so sharing their writing each day in an author chair just wasn't reasonable. This was when I decided to celebrate using an author day (see Figure 8.4). Essentially, this day is an entire class period where the final writing product of each student is placed onto the tables or desk. Students will come in and spend the day rotating in the classroom and reading their peers' writing.

These were the days that my students loved the most, even if writing wasn't their favorite subject. If that doesn't communicate the impact that an author's day has on students, then I am not sure what will. Besides exciting students, an author's day has many other benefits. The first is that it builds confidence in students as writers. When we share our work and receive praise (something that I discuss later in this chapter) it encourages us to feel pride in our work. Second, an author's day builds community. It allows us to encourage

Figure 8.4 Author's day celebration.

each other and gives way for conversations around how we are all in differ-ent spots in our learning. Every student's writing will look different and it helps us to develop understanding that we are diverse. Finally, an author's day provides closure to a writing unit. By having a day to celebrate and share our writing, it gives us purpose and solidifies the learning we've experienced over the last few weeks.

Implementing an Author's Day

As you work to determine when the best times are to incorporate an author's day, you'll want to consider a few components. The first is age; second and third graders might be able to complete a writing in two weeks while upper grades such as fourth through sixth grade take almost a month from planning to revisions and edits to complete a writing piece. You'll also want to look at your curriculum for guidance. I recommend an author's day for each type of writing. For my classroom, these are broken into writing units. We will have at least five author's days and sometimes six if we include a text dependent analysis. Decide where and when you want to hold an author's day and pencil these into your scope and sequence.

As mentioned, I use an author's day to bring closure to our writing units. While students are in the revision and editing phase, which takes around five to eight days, I inform them of when we will be holding our author's day. This builds anticipation and creates a deeper purpose for why they are writing. Typically, I meet with students during the revision process to give feedback, but I also have students work through a peer editing process. During this time, peers will look for punctuation, spelling, capitalization, and check for general understanding. For students who struggle a little more in writing, I sit down and help them through the editing process so that they feel confident when sharing their writing with their peers. Keep in mind that if you have many students that need support, you will need to take a few days to get this completed.

As students are finishing their writing, I have them use a personal printer that I keep in my classroom to print their final writing (see Figure 8.5).

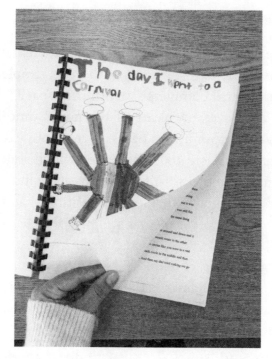

Figure 8.5 Publishing student work.

However, I understand that not every classroom has that capability. Think about how you will print student work or if you are going to have them hand-write their final, published, writing piece. Keep a checklist close by to mark off student writing as it is submitted. One management strategy I started was having a checklist for the writing process. At the start of every writing unit I would use this checklist to hold myself accountable for checking in with students throughout the unit.

Quick Tip: If you struggle to meet with all your students for each stage of the writing process, create groups of students and pull them as if you were pulling a small group. Have students work there and take out their writing so that you can quickly run through each students' work. Somehow when you pull a group of students one-on-one, you can get more accomplished in a shorter amount of time.

Making the Event Extra Special

Making an event extra special adds to the novelty and excitement of the day. While the day does not have to be over the top, simple touches such as music and decorations will completely transform a space. I have done a variation of author's days over my years of teaching; some have been short, sweet, simple, and to the point, and others were more extensive because of the decor and setup that I created. No matter which style you choose you can create an extra special day with touches that take little money and time. Here are some ideas to get you started in planning and making the day memorable:

- **Table covers and cafe music.** Transform your classroom by placing covers over the tables and desks. Add some café music at a low level in the background. You can find café scenery and music on YouTube that you can project and add to the ambiance.

- **Share popcorn and snacks!** Everyone loves food. I purchase large bags of popcorn and place them into cups for students to take their popcorn around the classroom. You can also bring other snacks if you don't love popcorn. Keep in mind students with allergies or braces. I will often have a selection of other snacks for them to eat and feel part of the community.

- **Have students make book covers.** Prior to the day, give students time to make book covers for their story. You can use a simple sheet of paper and have students add the title and their name as author on the cover. Don't have time in class? Give students the assignment during morning work or another time in class.

- **The power of sticky notes.** Place stacks of sticky notes around all the writing pieces in the classroom. As students finish reading, encourage them to leave a note detailing something they think the author did well or a part of the writing they loved the most. Students place the sticky note on the desk/table around the writing so that the author has something special to read when they come back to their seat. Remember to discuss the best comments to leave and comments they should stay away from; for example, I really liked your writing, isn't specific enough so you should say I really liked when Anna was in the forest and you described the scene.

Chapter Wrap-Up

Celebrating each other throughout the year creates some of my favorite memories as a classroom teacher. The smiles on their faces as their peers cheer them on and complement their work are the moments you will want to capture forever. They will bring you the strength to continue during difficult times and show you the importance of taking time from your teaching to celebrate your students. After reading this chapter, consider the following tips to guide you in implementing the new learning:

- Pencil in three to four days of teaching your students around the purpose of book talks.

- Decide on organizers or resources such as a sign-up calendar for students to use when creating their book talk.

- Have a location for students to gather resources and sign up for their book talk.

- Decide on when during the school day, or your literacy block, students can share their book talk,

- Decide on when to hold an author's day by considering holding one each month or at the end of a writing unit.

- Create a checklist to track students' writing to ensure everyone is prepared.

- Make the author's day event a little more special by sprinkling in some extra components.

9 | Come Together, Right Now

During my time in university, I had the pleasure to experience a variety of schools, classrooms, and grade levels. For my final internship I was placed in a third-grade classroom that would switch classes with another teacher in the building. I loved the experience because it opened my eyes to something very different than what I was used to, and it was with the two loveliest teachers one could ever hope to have as mentors. My one mentor teacher, Niki Burke, loved books and it reflected her decor and classroom library. I did as most young teachers do in the beginning: I asked tons of questions and made careful observations of how she structured her classroom. While I learned so many lessons from this teacher, for example, her caring heart for her students, her passion for teaching, her incredibly positive attitude, my biggest takeaway was her love for a read-aloud.

Each day, there was a special time in which we would enter the classroom. A student would pull the teacher's director's chair over from the corner of the classroom and place it center stage of the classroom. Then a book would be placed directly on the chair eager to be opened. Students would gather their snacks and water, and everyone would be seated facing the blue chair with her name stitched across the fabric. As she read, I watched as every student fixated on the story. I saw them react, whisper small words, and get excited to discuss the events that were unfolding. When her read-aloud time came to an end, the class would erupt with children saying "no!" and asking for her to continue reading more. That 15- to 20-minute block of time was special. It was a time for them all to feel united around a character and experience the story as a class.

Let me be clear on the read-aloud because the phrase can be loosely translated into different meanings. The read-aloud that I am referring to here is a time during your class period when you are reading a chapter book to your students. This doesn't mean that they all have individual copies of the book to follow along. In fact, I personally enjoyed giving students this time to enjoy a snack that they would bring from home. This time is all about reading for enjoyment and coming together with no added pressure to add a lesson or give additional work. It's about modeling to your class what it means to have meaningful conversations. Yes, we have read-alouds during our literacy blocks, and yes, we have conversations about those stories, but this is about getting engrossed in a novel and going through a larger journey. I've always steered away from using chapter books in my lessons because they take so much time and it can be easy to lose track of the story when you are modeling a strategy or skill. Therefore, having a separate time dedicated to a different type of reading was always essential in my own classroom.

That feeling stuck with me, and when I moved to kindergarten the following year, in that same building, I didn't start a chapter book read-aloud with my students. It just wasn't what the other kindergarten teachers were doing, and I was just trying to stay alive. My first year as a fourth-grade teacher changed all of that. I was so excited to incorporate a read-aloud time and have my students experience the same joy and excitement around a story. It became a sacred time in our class; we all came together, despite our different interests and friends, and united as a class (see Figure 9.1).

The longer I implemented a read-aloud time, the more I began to see the benefits that it had on my students and their learning. First is that it allowed students to hear a model reader. Before getting into this any further, I have to confess something; I did not start off as a great reader of chapter books. In fact, when my mentor teacher passed over the reading torch, I was

Figure 9.1 Reading aloud.

terrible. Becoming a good reader took time and lots of practice. I was able to be that good model for adding inflection and phrasing my words. I wasn't perfect, but I was able to show the authenticity of what it is like to read aloud. Students could connect with making mistakes and having days when your tongue felt tied. This opened doors to meaningful conversations that could help build confidence in their abilities as readers.

The next thing I realized was my students' willingness to have conversations about the story. This went beyond the conversations that happened during our mini-lessons; these were unstructured natural conversations that they initiated because they had so much passion for what was happening. I often found myself just sitting back and allowing them to discuss, predict, and infer various situations. I knew that what I was teaching them during our lessons was sticking; they just needed the right book to hone their instinct.

These conversations that my students were having eventually led them to build a stronger community of students. They learned to listen to each other's ideas, agree and disagree politely, and offer their own perspective based on their previous experiences. It allowed us to discuss empathy and create an environment where no one was judged, and all students were welcome. The lessons we learned from our read-alouds were authentic, not forced based on some required curriculum, and my students felt that. They took ownership of this time, and the 25 students who may not have always gotten along or played with each other at recess came together each day around a story.

Finally, I realized how much our read-alouds supported what we did in our lessons. Teaching students to take a chapter book that is much more complex and in-depth can feel overwhelming. I can still remember being the kid who paused every so often to count the pages I had left to read. As I mentioned, I refrained from ever using chapter books in my lessons, but I always understood the importance of teaching kids how to read chapter books. So, during my read-alouds, I get students to see the connections by bringing up lessons or making connections to other stories that we have read. When it came time to have my students get started with book clubs, using chapter books, they had already developed some sense of how to track their thinking and hold conversations about books. This unstructured time became an essential component to ensuring the success of my book clubs later.

Tips for Implementing a Read-Aloud

Maybe you're like me and you've always known that you've wanted a read-aloud time. You too wanted that undisrupted time to sit around, read a good book, and engage in conversations with your students. However, not every schedule allows for this time. I wanted to share some creative ways to go about trying to find a small 15- to 20-minute time that you can use in your block. If you are a teacher who switches blocks or has a partner teacher, then you might want to sit down and do this together. While you may not get the chance to do this in each of your blocks, you do have the ability to either:

(1) read to your homeroom class and your partner teacher reads to their class, or (2) everyone piles into your room, and you read it as a large group. Let's be honest, 15 minutes on the floor never hurt anyone.

Start by looking for a time away from your literacy block. Just because you are reading a book doesn't mean that it has to be connected to your ELA workshop. In fact, it is beneficial to find a separate time because it will be less likely that you will be disturbed by other happenings in the day. Look for times in your schedule where you have weird pockets of time. For example, one year I had a 15-minute block of time between recess and a special. I used this time to come in, cool down from recess and read our book. You might also be able to find time at the very end of the school day. My favorite read-aloud time was when I taught multiage. We had a 25-minute block from when we picked students up at special to when they started dismissal. It was a perfect time to gather everyone together to read a good book. Also keep in mind that if you have a crazy schedule that changes from day to day, you might be able to fit in more time on certain days of the week or in your cycle. Play around with the schedule until you find a system that works for you and your students.

Later in this chapter we are going to discuss how to choose the right book, but for now, I want to discuss the idea of having to read the book ahead of time. Some teachers are adamant that you must know the book you are going to read. I personally don't agree with this sentiment. There is something so special about experiencing a story line with your students. To feel the emotions for the first time and allow your students to see your reaction is what helps to spark their own interest in the story. Have I had times when a story hasn't worked out the way I wanted it to? Yes, and there is nothing wrong with expressing this sentiment with your students. When I read the book *The Wild Robot* by Peter Brown for the first time, I remember there being a moment when I put the book down and told my class that I was really struggling to get into the story. The same situation happened when I read *Echo Mountain* by Lauren Wolk with my class, but instead of quitting, we talked about what we were feeling as readers and we agreed to persevere.

I was able to model what to do when you are not interested in a book. These lessons are the ones my students will always remember because they were real.

Once you get started with your readings, you'll want to find authentic ways to create meaningful connections. I am not a fan of using this time to create more work for your students. Remember, learning should be simple and authentic. Instead of constantly throwing worksheets or questionnaires at your class, get them thinking with simple phrases such as: "Who remembers the story we read where the character was faced with a similar conflict?" or "I want you to pause and notice how the author describes this section of the story. What do you think the author does really well?" Nothing too flashy or extensive, but simple enough to get students thinking. The more you can connect what you are teaching to the story you are reading, the more your students will develop that connection as well.

If while you are reading you want to create an authentic and interactive experience with the text, there are a few strategies that might be worth mentioning. These are ideas that I have explored in the past. I don't force myself to do these activities all the time, but instead keep these resources close by so that I can utilize them to facilitate conversations. Here are some basic ideas that you can easily implement and some that might take extra prep time but have a big impact on your students:

- **Create a read–aloud tracker.** Teaching students to understand and identify the elements of plot within a larger text can be challenging. To give students plenty of experience with how to develop this skill, create a plot mountain on your bulletin board and track the events of the story as you read it with your class. You can have a more elaborate setup as shown in Figure 9.2 or you can use sticky notes that can be added to an anchor chart.
- **Have students stop and jot during meaningful moments.** Get students to share their thinking on paper by having them do a stop-and-jot on an index card, sticky note, or notebook. This can be in response to an event that happened or how a character has responded to a big moment

Figure 9.2 Read-aloud tracker.

in the text. After giving students time to write their thoughts, have learners share some of their responses.

- **Use interactive activities such as Book, Head, Heart, or Signposts.** Give students a meaningful way to develop connections between events that are happening in the book and their personal lives with physical signs that they can raise when a thought arises. I have used Book, Head, Heart which is a concept from the book *Disrupting Thinking*, and Signposts from the book *Notice & Note* both by Kylene Beers and Robert E. Probst.

- **Have students share their thoughts in discussion boards, reading responses, and more.** As the year progresses and you'd like to scaffold the times students share, you can begin to incorporate days when students respond more formally through discussion boards (see Figure 9.3), reading responses, and analyzing specific elements of the text. If you can, hand out photocopies of the paragraph or page that you want students to reference. This will especially encourage students to pull evidence from the text to support their thinking.

- **Find creative ways to make a connection.** There will be some books that lend themselves to more creative methods for interacting with the

Figure 9.3 Discussion question in Schoology or Projector.

story line. Take the book *Nightbooks* by J.A. White in which the character writes scary stories that are read throughout the book. You can have students finish the stories shared in their own writing during your literacy block or for morning work. Give students an opportunity to share their writing with the class. Another example is the book *Fish in a Tree* by Lynda Mullaly Hunt. The main character Ally has a sketchbook of impossible things. Have students create their own sketchbook of impossible things. As Ally shares various scenarios have students sketch out what they visualize and share their drawings with the class.

Choosing the Right Books

I remember spending days trying to decide on the best read-aloud. I always wanted it to be better than the last to hook my students and leave them wanting more. Everyone has their own thoughts on which book is the best to start with, and why they love it, but we have to remember that books hold special meanings to us all. We remember the stories we read because the character or storyline resonates with us. While you might think picking the perfect read-aloud book is hard, it is a much easier process than you think. Start by looking for books that will build conversations. You can do a simple Google search or spend some time reading the back covers of books in the library or your local bookstore. Oftentimes, I enjoy choosing books that I think students might relate to, and this typically involves a character that is in school going through typical issues that can be found in almost every classroom. *Fish in a Tree* is a great example of a book that naturally builds conversations because the character Ally has a learning disability.

You can also choose books that explore the variations in the types of texts by picking various genres for your read-alouds. I like to choose, at minimum, a realistic fiction, a fantasy text, and a historical fiction book to read each year. Recently, I took a leap of faith and decided to talk to my class about reading a book written in verse. I spoke to them about my apprehension of reading this type of book aloud and we all agreed to give it a try. I read *The Canyon's Edge* by Dusti Bowling, and my students were completely enthralled by the action of each scene. They enjoyed talking about how the author told the stories through poetry, and more importantly, the way the poems sometimes gave way to the meaning of the story from the designs. The entire experience opened my eyes to the possibilities of including other forms of novels. Simply by using this strategy, we can hold meaningful discussions about how we approach understanding the story, setting, and characters depending on the genre we are reading.

Another strategy for choosing books is to focus on the content you are teaching during your literacy block. If you are focusing on characters, then look for stories that contain strong characters and experience some form of a change. The book *Wish* by Barbara O'Connor revolves around a young girl who is going through a difficult time. She has internal and external conflict that she struggles with throughout the story, only to resolve all her problems at the very end. If you've had an opportunity to teach both literature and information, locate a historical fiction book that will allow you to pull informational articles to analyze as a class. You can choose to do this during your morning work or literacy block, and make references to your read-aloud.

I would like to bring up books that are written in a series. Some good examples of these are the *Land of Stories* by Chris Colfer, *Gregor the Overlander* by Suzanne Collins, and more. As much as you'd think that reading these books in sequence would be a great (and easy) way of choosing books for your read-aloud, I'd like to add a few words of caution. Books in a series, while great for hooking students into the story line and encouraging them to continue reading, should not be used during this time unless you are reading the first book in the series to help encourage reluctant readers. An example of this is when I read the book *A Tale Dark and Grimm* by Adam Gidwitz. This book hooked every student in my classroom, and while picking up the second book in the series would have been an easy selection, I gathered the books and displayed them for students to continue the tale independently. Reading the same story doesn't give your students experience with a variety of texts and storylines. Use these books to encourage additional reading, not consume your read-aloud time.

If it comes down to a select few books that you simply cannot bear to decide between, don't. Get your students involved in the process of selecting the class read-aloud by holding a voting session. To prepare for this, I gather the

Figure 9.4 Book voting.

books and we spend one to two days reading the back of each book, discussing the covers, and even reading the first few pages of each book. If I can find a book trailer on each book online, then I will also show these to the class. At the end, I create a Google Form or have a physical voting system for students to pick their favorite (see Figure 9.4). I announce the winner and we celebrate. This is a simple way to model to students how to select books, and it makes students feel more invested in the book they chose to read.

Chapter Wrap-Up

Building a love of reading with your students is a powerful experience. Hopefully after reading this chapter, you've realized that it doesn't have to be done by increasing a student's reading fluency, teaching skills, and strategies for analyzing a text. Teaching students to love reading can be as simple as those unstructured opportunities that we give our students to come together and enjoy a story as a class. While all the previous chapters define the structure of your block and give you the necessary strategies for building independent readers and writers, it is through the reading of a book and the conversations that stem from it that your students will remember the most. Yes, we have to collect data and make sure our students are growing, but don't forget the real reason why you chose to be a reading and writing teacher: to help spread the love of reading. After reading this chapter, consider the following tips to guide you in implementing the new learning:

- Look through your schedule and block out a time for your read-aloud.
- Select the first book that you will read to your students.
- Decide on how you will track the books you read this year.
- Create small opportunities for your students to interact and engage with the text and their peers.

Conclusion

It's the Final Countdown

Each year, our classrooms change ever so slightly. We try new designs. We implement new strategies, or we make our space feel fresh. This keeps us developing and enjoying what we do. Sometimes we must make changes for the good of our students despite how we feel. This was the case for me.

After a decade of teaching, I moved to a new school. I felt like a solid teacher, especially in reading and writing. I didn't expect this to be a problem with my experience and skills. It shocked me that the first four months at this new school were some of the most challenging times I ever experienced in teaching. Set in my ways, I expected these strategies to continue working for this new group of learners. In my heart, I knew these were the best ways to teach reading and writing. At the end of those four months, I finally realized that maybe things needed to change in order to fit the needs of my students.

I went back to the drawing board and carefully considered everything that I was doing in my classroom. What was working for my students? What needs was I not meeting? I made some accommodations, but I wanted to stay true to my beliefs. My fourth-grade classroom ranged with an array of needs. I had students who needed basic blends and vowel patterns, students who needed fluency and retelling, and those who were performing at their grade level. I couldn't meet the needs of all those students while teaching one mini-lesson. Did I mention that I only had about 75 minutes to teach reading and writing? That factor alone made things more challenging.

After lots of time debating and reworking, I concluded I had to stop putting both of my blocks into the same box. I had a morning class and an afternoon class. Both had their own unique needs. I wanted to keep them the same, but I wondered why. The answer was because it was easier for me as a teacher. I started considering what it might look like if I only taught using small groups. I conducted my mini-lesson four separate times during the class period. This process would allow me to structure each lesson based on the needs of the group. For example, I introduced one group to the vowel pattern of the week and had a sort and introduction to their decodable. Another group would begin working on a reading strategy. The third needed more scaffolding to read the passage to increase their fluency and understanding, before moving on to the reading skill. Though I created multiple lessons per day, each lesson was more intentional.

The story is about taking risks. If we don't look for new possibilities, we won't change. Our flexibility as teachers makes us excel at our jobs. It allows us to look for new ways of approaching situations and adapting when we least expect it. My situation forced me to adapt and make adjustments for my students. I realized that my instruction was not reaching all of my learners; and instead of complaining or leaving frustrated each day, I took what I knew, and I tweaked it ever so slightly. As you read through this book, you probably thought, "There's no way this would work for me" or "My students are not independent enough for this structure." I challenge you to tweak these ideas to make them fit you and your students.

This book won't solve all your problems. Nothing is perfect. If there was a system that worked for every classroom and every student then we would all have a perfect literacy block. However, if we dwell on trying to build this image of perfection to grow, we will quickly lose our joy that led us to this profession.

A superintendent of mine once said, "Fail forward." When we fail, look at the failure as an opportunity to learn. We accept our inability to grow in our profession when we choose to not try because of the fear of failure. When we fail forward, we work toward progress. Will you choose to fail forward?

Making the Most of This Book

Have you attended a professional development where you got a full day of information? You are excited to teach, but unsure where to start. This eventually results in nothing happening because the thought of doing everything is too overwhelming to even consider. This happens to me when I attend professional developments or even after reading a book. Instead of simply dismissing everything you've just read in this book, there are ways that can help make putting these ideas into practice much more manageable. On the following pages, you will find some reminders that can guide you through this process and see a shift in your literacy block. If you've read the information to his point but don't start taking action, you are choosing to not grow and solve the struggles you are experiencing. It will make your life easier later if you work hard now. Would you rather struggle for a little or struggle for what seems like eternity?

Start Small and Grow

Think back to goals that you may have set for yourself. What goals were they? When did you set the deadline for the goal? Every year I would make a goal to drink more water and cut out Diet Coke® completely. I start off strong and quickly find defeat after only a couple of weeks. Why did this happen? One reason was that my ambition was too big. I was setting myself up for failure before I had even gotten started. We take time to scaffold goals, assignments, and new learning for our students. We must do the same for our teaching practices. Use the steps below as a guide.

Step 1: Open up a blank Google Doc or take out a sheet of blank paper. Set a timer for about 30 minutes to one hour and reflect on your current practices. Use these questions as a guide: In which areas am I the strongest? Which areas should I improve? Am I meeting the needs of my students? If not, which students would I like to improve their instruction? These are just the starting point; you can dig deeper in each focus area of your instruction. Keep these focused on your literacy block.

Step 2: After reflecting, take some time to identify similarities between the areas that you feel as though are a weakness in your instruction. For example, if you wrote you struggle with work for independent activities, and you struggle with behavior management while students are independent, those two can have a direct correlation in that your independent time needs more structure. This will weed through your list and give you a specific focus.

Step 3: Now that you have your key areas of focus, place them in order of importance. Identify the areas that represent the 20% that will bring 80% of growth, as discussed in Chapter 1. For example, if your list contains mini-lesson instruction, read alouds, and engagement, you might choose mini-lessons as your first focus, engagement as your second, and then read alouds.

Step 4: Look back at the chapters that correspond to your focus area. Decide the strategies or steps you are going to take, and begin creating an action plan. This means setting dates that are aligned with your goals. Keep a reasonable number of goals and strategies to implement. Start small and grow.

The process that I have laid out will keep you focused and driven to slowly building improvement in your instruction. I caution teachers from having too many goals in the beginning. I suggest you start with one goal and give yourself time to implement strategies. Once you feel comfortable with your goal, then you can reflect and add new goals.

Adjust When Needed

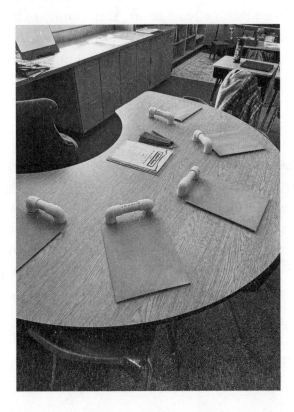

When I first went into teaching, blogging and social media were just taking off. This made me even more excited to dedicate myself to the profession. However, I wanted nothing more than to replicate what other teachers were doing online. In wanting to be like these teachers, I lost who I was. When I came upon this realization, I made minor adjustments. This meant that I changed around my lessons by making it work for my personality. I thought about my needs and determined which practices best fit what I was already doing well in the classroom. This process gave me the ability to create a literacy block that I loved.

The strategies and ideas that are shared throughout this book are simple teaching practices. However, you do not need to do them exactly as I have described. I found that doing what others have done to find a method that works best for me was helpful on my journey, but I never intended on doing it the same way for the remainder of my career. Steal the methods that are described in this book, and as you implement them, look for adjustments that fit your style of teaching after you have had some time to truly understand the purpose and results you desire. You'll find something that works for you. I suggest implementing new strategies for at least three months before placing your spin on things. You will feel more confident and aware of what your students need.

Listen to the Needs of Your Students

Every year, we eagerly await our new group of learners. With the change of our rosters, the dynamics, personalities, and needs also change. Then why do our lesson plans and formats stay exactly the same each year? Without listening to the needs of my students and being open with reevaluating my practices, I would never have tailored their learning experiences. This process allowed my students to grow academically as both readers and writers, but it also gave me the opportunity to grow professionally.

You are probably asking yourself, "But how do I go about doing this?" The answer is complex. Take the first quarter of the school year and learn about your students. Track their strengths, weaknesses, and their interests during those first nine weeks. Determining the changes that need to be made depends on this timeframe. Don't feel as though you have to start the year making adjustments. Once you have a better understanding of their needs, you can go back and ask the questions at the start of this chapter.

There Is No One Way

You know the route to work, but I want you to consider the route your coworkers take. Is this the same or different? Even if your coworker lives next door, they'd still have a slightly longer or shorter route, making every person's drive unique. There is no one way to get to work or teach literacy. Every person's path is unique and based on their own preferences and circumstances. When we consider the work that other teachers are doing in their classrooms, we must also consider the path that they prefer. How will you tailor your instruction to match your path?

There are always approaches, wording, and systems that can still give you the same results without compromising your unique teaching style. For example, you might prefer to display your learning targets in a morning message or on your anchor charts, while I have mine posted on my board for students to reference. Does the placement of the learning target matter for students' learning? It does not. The results will be the same if you implement it into your instruction. You bring attention to the focus of the lesson and building independence, and that's what is important. You can take what I present in this book and make it better based on your unique perspectives.

If you've highlighted and found strategies you've implemented from this book, try to implement it how I have shared. Think about changes you can make. Perhaps you've read something in the book that you like some parts of, but others don't seem like they will fit with the requirements set forth by your school. Here, ask yourself whether there are parts of the strategy that you can implement.

Your Ideal Literacy Block

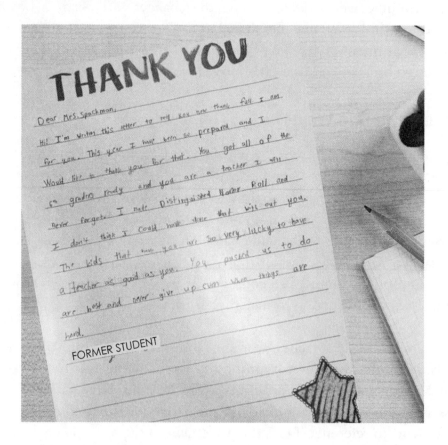

Thinking back to when I first started teaching upper elementary, I always knew that I wanted to build a literary block that would inspire my students. I wanted to create an environment in which students felt comfortable and excited about opening their books. I wanted to create thoughtful thinkers who would discuss rich texts and apply their learning to their writing. More than anything, I wanted my students to love reading and writing. Creating this space was never linear. My journey took turns, loops, and full 360s as I recognized what authentic and rigorous teaching practices look like.

Your literacy block will continue to develop throughout your career. Even today, I find new improvements, approaches, and alternatives for meeting the needs of my students. Thinking that your literacy block will be exactly what you want or expect it to be is a utopian idea. Once you have one area mastered, you'll find yourself with an entirely new group of students who make what you've implemented in the past unrealistic. Is there an ideal literacy block? My answer is both no and yes. No, it is impossible to pinpoint your ideal literacy block because we are forever changing. Ideal means having everything your heart desires, and we always wish for more time, more resources, and more support. Yes, you can find your ideal literacy block so long as you will reflect and revise your practices. There is such a thing as coming into your classroom and feeling like you've put forth your best effort to meet the needs of your students.

My hope for you is that this book has inspired you to create a literacy block that checks off all the wants on your list. I hope you find value in the information and learning that I gained as an upper elementary teacher. While I cannot promise you victory toward your ideal literacy block, I hope this book gives you the steps to get closer. Just remember the reason you teach reading and writing. It isn't wanting students to perform well on the state test or to leave on a specific reading level by the end of the year. We become teachers to make a difference in the lives of our students. We want to help guide them to the impact that reading and writing will have on their lives. If you do the work, students will forever remember the impact you made.

Acknowledgments

It's something special to find a partner in life that supports you in everything you want to do. Thank you to my amazing husband who has sacrificed so much to lift me up. Your support, and love has motivated me to strive for big goals and dreams. You are always there when I need words of encouragement or to push me to see new perspectives. You've given me the tough words when I needed to hear them and pushed me to always better myself. You always give so much to everyone around you, and I am beyond lucky to have you as my husband and father of our two boys. Cheers, to many more years.

I also want to thank my two boys, Ian and Blaine. You both have done nothing but inspire me to be better in so many ways. Without your smiles, hugs, and laughs, my life would be nothing. I hope you know that so much of what I do in my work is to make sure that you have a better future. You are both my world, and I love you more than words can describe.

To my best friend and business partner, Michelle Emerson. Thank you for always supporting my crazy ideas and telling me when I should probably step back. Thank you for giving me the tough love necessary and the guidance for navigating this crazy, amazing world we have created for ourselves. You have always, and continue, to inspire me through your own work and creativity. I am so thankful to that little business trip that brought us both together.

To my cousin, Juan Edgar Gonzalez Jr., you are an inspiration and calming soul to everyone around you. Your passion for literacy instruction and your laid back personality brings a smile to my face. I have been so fortunate to have been on this journey of life with you. I've grown up with you, and watched the hardships you have faced and how you never allowed it to impact your viewpoint on life. Thank you for the constant conversations after school, our writer's retreat, and for the hours of laughter.

To my mom and dad, Maria and Nomi Yusafi. Your commitment and dedication to not only your work, but also your family is a constant model for what I want to achieve in my lifetime. You both make such a difference in people's lives and to watch how loved and respected you both are is truly inspiring. Thank you for your guidance, support, and for being the best grandparents. I am beyond lucky to have you both in my life, and I am so grateful for all the times you were so tough on me as a teenager. Who would have ever thought that I would be an author!

To my in-laws, Dan and Kelli Spackman. From the very beginning you opened your home to me. I have learned so much from your guidance these past years, and I hope you both know how much I love and respect you. Thank you for bringing my husband into my life, thank you for opening your home to me, and thank you for being amazing grandparents. I could not have made it through this book or any other project without your love and support.

My friend, Lesley Carmichael, it is truly a remarkable thing to have such a close friend and yet we have never met in real life. At some point we will need to solve this problem. Thank you for always being so supportive of everything I do. Your honesty and passion for wanting to make a difference in education is contagious. Thank you for the long phone calls, the quick text check-ins, and always being my cheerleader. Anyone who has you as a friend is incredibly lucky!

Finally, but most certainly not least, to all the teachers who have pushed to make a change in education, especially those who are in my Bridging Literacy Community. It is because of all of you that the face of what literacy instruction looks like in upper elementary is changing. Your dedication to making an authentic, fun, and rigorous environment is what helps to create a better future for our children. As a mother and fellow educator I want to thank you for working through the noise and focusing on what is important. It is because of you all that teaching reading and writing is fun. Keep doing what you love, keep sharing, and keep speaking out to make a better space for literacy instruction.

Index

Page numbers followed by *f* refer to figures.